A Place Calling Itself Rome

by the same author

LOOK BACK IN ANGER
THE ENTERTAINER

with Anthony Creighton
EPITAPH FOR GEORGE DILLON

THE WORLD OF PAUL SUCKEY
A SUBJECT OF SCANDAL AND CONCERN
LUTHER
PLAYS FOR ENGLAND:
The Blood of the Bambergs and *Under Plain Cover*
UNDER PLAIN COVER
INADMISSIBLE EVIDENCE
A PATRIOT FOR ME
A BOND HONOURED
TIME PRESENT AND THE HOTEL IN AMSTERDAM
TOM JONES: A film script
THE RIGHT PROSPECTUS: A Play for Television
VERY LIKE A WHALE
WEST OF SUEZ
HEDDA GABLER adapted from Henrik Ibsen
THE GIFT OF FRIENDSHIP: A Play for Television
A SENSE OF DETACHMENT

JOHN OSBORNE

A Place Calling Itself Rome

FABER AND FABER
3 Queen Square
London

First published in 1973
by Faber and Faber Limited
3 Queen Square London WC1
Printed in Great Britain by
Unwin Brothers Limited
Old Woking Surrey GU22 9LH

ISBN 0 571 10277 8 (hard bound edition)
ISBN 0 571 10278 6 (paper covers)

All applications for professional and amateur rights
should be addressed to Margery Vosper Ltd.,
53a Shaftesbury Avenue, London, W.1.

CAST

CAIUS MARCIUS, afterwards CAIUS MARCIUS CORIOLANUS

TITUS LARTIUS ⎫
COMINIUS ⎭ generals against the Volscians

MENENIUS AGRIPPA, friend to Coriolanus

SICINIUS VELUTUS ⎫
JUNIUS BRUTUS ⎭ Tribunes

YOUNG MARCIUS, son to Coriolanus

TULLUS AUFIDIUS, general of the Volscians

LIEUTENANTS TO AUFIDIUS

FOLLOWERS OF AUFIDIUS

ROMAN PARATROOPER

RADIO SIGNALLER

MAN IN ANTIUM PUB

VOLUMNIA, mother to Coriolanus

VIRGILIA, wife to Coriolanus

VALERIA, friend to Virgilia

SERVANT TO VOLUMNIA

ROMAN AND VOLSCIAN SOLDIERS, SENATORS,
CITIZENS, MESSENGERS, POLICE OFFICERS, MEDICAL
ORDERLIES, OFFICIALS, PATRICIANS, AEDILE (OR
PEOPLE'S POLICEMAN), ATTENDANTS AND MOB.

The action takes place in Rome, Corioli and Antium.

Act One

SCENE ONE

Rome. The bedroom of CAIUS MARCIUS. *He lies beside his wife* VIRGILIA, *staring at the first light as it begins to cut more clearly across the bed. He cries out, half waking.*

CORIOLANUS: Corioli! Aufidius!
VIRGILIA: What?
CORIOLANUS: Corioli!
VIRGILIA: Um. (*She turns to lie on his neck*) Sh!
CORIOLANUS: What?
VIRGILIA: Dreaming.
CORIOLANUS: Yes . . .
VIRGILIA: What time is it?
CORIOLANUS: Early. Go back to sleep.
VIRGILIA: So it is. I will. You woke me with your 'Aufidius' and and your 'Corioli'.
CORIOLANUS: I'm sorry.
VIRGILIA: And you.
CORIOLANUS: I will . . . Virgilia . . .
VIRGILIA: What is it? It's so early! What's about Corioli? And Aufidius? Where are you going?
CORIOLANUS: Nowhere. Sleep.
   (*She turns over and he kisses her.*)
VIRGILIA: You're not to go to old Corioli.
CORIOLANUS: No. You're right. Not for the while. (*He pats her hair and goes to the window*) Does the light disturb you?
   (*She makes no answer but her heavy breathing returns soon.*)
   I'll close this bit of curtain . . .
   (*He sits at a table and switches on a tiny light which serves to isolate his wife in more darkness. Taking out a notebook, he writes in an unsure hand.*)

Concentration difficult. More so today. Woke suddenly. Foot almost through the sheet. Today more difficult . . . sure to. Senate . . . people . . . crowds. Tribunes and all of that! No chance of waking *her* again. . . . A few more hours. . . . And years, not years. Surely. Things in flight on first waking. . . . Flying blind. Blind flying. No pilot beside. Just as well. . . . Decisions impossible. But *forced* ones. Elephants of decisions. Over-weighted. Jostled. . . . Crowds. . . . Hold back. . . . But how? (*To* VIRGILIA) Am I disturbing you?

(*No answer.*)

Mind racing but no engine. Body concentrates, then flies off. Women. Thoughts of women. All of them. More all the time. Can't write, die to write . . . *dictate* . . . Sex flickers, no flame. What to even consider. To do. Coherent? No. Speech even surprisingly blurred. Early. But Senate. Crowds. Hold back. And not just by morning. No, not later . . . later. Tears far too close, close too hard. At bedside. Rising After Rising Use After Tears! Absurdities, lying *aware*. By the bath. Locked in. One hour. Half. Twenty minutes. Six. Don't. No further. *Don't* get light. No light. Bother? Rightly? Power without storage. Eaten little. Four, no, what, five days. Up. Thrown up. Slime, squalid slime on beard and towels. Musn't let it be shown. Laundry. *They* know. No. They—don't. Bath. Dread the water. Teeth unclean but nothing will trick *them* up. Mustn't. Bed. Got an hour. No. Fifty minutes . . . Drank That much. Did I? No. Yes . . . No. What action! Action? Just spectacle. Bombast . . . Wrote to my mother. Wrote? I made marks. Perhaps she will die? No. She won't. She's young. Younger than I. That's for certain.

VIRGILIA: Come back to bed.

CORIOLANUS: Coming.

VIRGILIA: Do you want to talk?

CORIOLANUS: No.

VIRGILIA: Eat?

CORIOLANUS: No. But thank you.

VIRGILIA (*returning to supine position*): You must be tired.

CORIOLANUS: Yes.

VIRGILIA: *I* am.

(*He starts getting back to bed, turning off the lamp and so on.*)

CORIOLANUS: You must be. (*Hums*)

> The working class
> Can kiss my arse.
> Just Keep the Red
> Rags up, flying high.

(*He settles into bed.*)

VIRGILIA (*drowsy*): Why are you singing?

CORIOLANUS: I'm not. With words is . . .

VIRGILIA: What?

CORIOLANUS: Words is that they, that is, people, expect them to mean either what they say, don't say, or may say . . .

VIRGILIA: People?

CORIOLANUS: The people. Goodnight.

VIRGILIA: Good morning . . . Cuddle . . .

(*Soon there is the sound only of her breath.* CORIOLANUS *lies in the darkness, then puts on a gown and goes out, leaving the soft sound and darkness.*)

SCENE TWO

Rome. A street. Light flashes on, dazzling after first scene. The Roman mob enters. Also police and some troops, discreetly dressed. Note: Mob scenes, demonstrations and so on are obviously up to the director's resources, lack of them, taste, inclination, disinclination or lack of it. However, after the dawn unease of the preceding scene, I would suggest something of the following as a pattern for the similar scenes in the play: a cross-section MOB *of* STUDENTS, FIXERS, PUSHERS, POLICEMEN, UNIDENTIFIABLE PUBLIC, *obvious* TRADE UNIONISTS, JOURNALISTS *and the odd* NEWS CAMERA TEAM, SOUND MEN, *etc., shrills of police horses, linked arms on all sides; screaming girls, banners of the nineteenth-century sort, banners of the modern kind—*'CAIUS MARCIUS: GO FUCK YOURSELF'; 'WE WANT A LAY NOT DELAY'; 'ONE QUARTER OWNS THREE-QUARTERS'; 'NO MORE TRIX JUST A FIX'; *the head of a pig with* 'CAIUS MARCIUS' *inscribed on it;* 'CAIUS MARCIUS IS THE BERK—LET HIM GO

AND DO THE WORK'; *Roman troops can be in flak jackets and helmets. Patricians like M.P.s or high-ranking officers. The* VOLSCIANS *more revolutionary in appearance but still often martial, with berets and insignia, etc. When the Roman mob enters, it can be chanting for example:* AU-FID-IUS.

MOB: AUFIDIUS—AU-FID-IUS—AU-FID-IUS!
　　　(*Laughter, jeers. A flag is burnt centre stage and waved aloft. Banners wave, stones, marbles thrown. Hand-clapping; cheers. A pop group possibly joins in for a while. The chaos and noise is eventually brought under the partial control of the* FIRST CITIZEN.)
1ST CITIZEN: Hear me! Will you listen to me!
MOB: Go on then. (*etc.*)
1ST CITIZEN: We are all, all of us resolved, determined——
VOICE: Get on with it!
1ST CITIZEN: To die, yes, if we have to, rather than put up with this state of things.
VOICE: What state of things!
1ST CITIZEN: What state of things he says!
VOICE: Caius Marcius!
　　　(ROAR.)
1ST CITIZEN: Is that not 'state of things' enough for you!
VOICE: More than enough, if you ask me!
MOB: CAIUS MARCIUS OUT! MARCIUS OUT! OUT ! OUT! MARCIUS OUT!
1ST CITIZEN: Then what's the answer!
VOICE: We know the answer all right.
1ST CITIZEN: Haven't we got teeth then!
VOICE: Yours look as if you'd got 'em for nothing!
　　　(LAUGHTER.)
1ST CITIZEN: Then let's *use* 'em!
MOB: Use 'em!
2ND CITIZEN: A word, my good friends!
VOICE: A word, he says. We've had enough bleeding words!
　　　(CHEERS.)
1ST CITIZEN: Don't 'good friends' us—my good friends! The patricians call you 'my good friend' every day. And why? Because they can *afford* to!
　　　(APPLAUSE.)

14

We aren't their 'good friends'. *We're* too expensive! Are you still taken in by this patronage and soft sell and big dealing for other people? Yes, *others*. And what others? People who were best off dead and long ago. I know this, you know this, and we know it, and because it's there to be seen, seen in us, in us, and not some daft, obsolete, self-perpetuating senate.

(ROAR.)

2ND CITIZEN: Tell me. No, let me say something a moment.

VOICE: Give a chance!

2ND CITIZEN: Why do you single out Caius Marcius? Why? Why pick on him?

1ST CITIZEN: Single out! Do you hear that! *Pick* on Caius *Marcius*!

(SHOUTS.)

2ND CITIZEN: Well, why?

1ST CITIZEN: Because he *is:* is a Pig.

(ROAR.)

And of all pigs, the piggiest of 'em all.

(LOUDER ROAR.)

2ND CITIZEN: So *you* say.

VOICE: So say all of *us*!

(CHEERS *etc.*)

2ND CITIZEN: Don't you think he's done something, cared something——

1ST CITIZEN: For him*self*.

2ND CITIZEN: His country.

VOICE: Somebody *do* him. (*etc.*)

1ST CITIZEN: That's all past.

2ND CITIZEN: What is! Past.

1ST CITIZEN: What I said: everything.

VOICE: You heard: all!

2ND CITIZEN: All!

MOB: All. (*etc.*)

2ND CITIZEN: Isn't there any memory left! Just malice!

MOB: Get out of it, get stuffed. (*etc.*)

1ST CITIZEN: He served his time, such as it was. *And*, mark you, his wife, his mother, his child, his fine houses, his horses.

2ND CITIZEN: Is a man who keeps his wife, child, a horse, a house: a traitor, some—a backslider or something!

1ST CITIZEN: Yes.

MOB: Yes.

(ROAR.)

2ND CITIZEN: He's had little more than most——

1ST CITIZEN: So. Is that all the good you can find in him?

VOICE: Exploiter.

(ROAR.)

1ST CITIZEN: The Pigs are rising. Then let's go and meet them. The Capitol!

MOB: The Capitol!

(*They poise to go as* MENENIUS *enters, surrounded by a discreet guard of* POLICEMEN *and* PLAIN CLOTHES MEN.)

2ND CITIZEN: Menenius! You can't say *he's* not honest! Even for a patrician, would you say he's devious?

VOICE: Devious! No. Drunk more likely!

(ROAR.)

MENENIUS: What's this, lads! Banners, police, stones, trampling——

VOICE: Affray!

MENENIUS: Ah—do I hear a legal mind?

VOICE: You have to be in this lark!

MENENIUS: Speak up then. You!

1ST CITIZEN: The Senate is not exactly unaware of our existence.

VOICE: Too many of us by now.

(ROAR.)

1ST CITIZEN: They've known a fortnight what we'll do. And now they'll see it really happen!

MENENIUS: My good friends . . .

VOICE: Good friends!

(GROANS. BOOS.)

MENENIUS: Will you ruin the life you've got?

1ST CITIZEN: What life?

MENENIUS: Then the life you're going to have.

VOICE: We've heard *that* a few times.

MENENIUS: I still say: the life you *shall* HAVE!

(*A few cheers; some boos and disturbances; he manages to gain attention.*)

Shall have! I say it again. *Shall.*

VOICE: I'll bet. What about *us*.

(*'What about us' etc.;* MENENIUS *waits for them to subside; hand-clapping, etc.*)

MENENIUS: Shall I speak or not?

1ST CITIZEN: No.

MOB: No.

1ST CITIZEN: Textbook oratory! There is no room in revolution for impartial leaders.

MOB: Pig! Pigs! Pet the Pigs!

2ND CITIZEN: Where's custom then? Is there no virtue left?

1ST CITIZEN: No!

2ND CITIZEN: Precedent?

1ST CITIZEN: Don't appeal to precedent. Or we shall *all* die.

MOB: Dead! Dead!

2ND CITIZEN: And Virtue.

1ST CITIZEN: What's that then?

MOB: Yes, what's that then?

MENENIUS: The Riddle of Change, my good friend.

2ND CITIZEN: 'The Riddle of Change'. Is *that* what it is! It'll make a footnote for you. Where's Caius Marcius?

(*He goes out but not without man-handling by the mob. Or sections of it.*)

MENENIUS: I appeal to you!

VOICE: Oh, no, you don't.

(LAUGHTER.)

(MENENIUS *lurches on.*)

MENENIUS: I beg you—let him go. He *is* one of us, whatever you may say.

VOICE: And *you.*

MENENIUS: We *are* you!

1ST CITIZEN: Come off it!

MENENIUS: I will not come off it. As I've always done.

(*Some* CHEERS.)

We are for *you*, we are *yours*, you can rid yourselves of us, whenever you wish! When*ever.* But what then?

1ST CITIZEN: Then we'll see!

(CHEERS.)

MENENIUS: But what? We Romans have a surplus of emotion all right. But what else? Do we have a surplus of *trade*?

VOICE: When did *I* work last then?

MENENIUS: Right, my good friend. But do you think no one cares for you? Why do you only bait and assault the ones who care the most for you?

1ST CITIZEN: What care did you ever have for us!

MENENIUS: Think of our efforts!

1ST CITIZEN: I'd rather not.

VOICE: More shooting and 'tighten your belts' and a bit off the taxes.

1ST CITIZEN: If you're lucky.

VOICE: Fine fucking *effort*!

(ROAR.)

1ST CITIZEN: I've heard enough.

MENENIUS: Rome must be a city worth saving *for*. Not in the next month. But the years to come.

VOICE: What about the meantime!

MENENIUS: It will be as *mean* and ready as you choose to make it.

1ST CITIZEN: Easy laugh!

MENENIUS: We must have faith, confidence.

VOICE: *You're* all right, mate. What about today?

MENENIUS: And *I* say, what of tomorrow? Be patient——

1ST CITIZEN: While you spout?

MENENIUS: And what else do *you* do, my good friend.

VOICE: Yes, What does *he* do!

(ROAR.)

MENENIUS: Very well then, We are on the threshold of a new experience. Let's embrace it, it and a Rome worth working for. When you talk of revolution so easily, so do I, so do *I*. I see the revolution of rising expectations. That—that is what concerns the Senate, your Senate. For what else is it? We must reconcile all expectations and try to disappoint none. We may fail in some but we will *succeed* in some. A note of steady expansion. We'll not flinch. No, not from that. But there must be decision making too. We must be a true *community*. For us in the Senate there is a special challenge.

Not simply of book-making, of *priorities*. Major *Policies*.
Policies. Policies!
(*His voice is drowned in the chorus of* 'POLICIES'.)
There may be new methods, new machinery of government.
Some untested, not even installed. As I told you we Romans
have a surplus of *emotion*. What do the others have? A
surplus of *trade*!
(CHEERS.)
Different hopes to reconcile. People will save for homes, but
where shall they be built? But they will be built! They will
save for journeys to strange places and time to enjoy. Young
marrieds, elder citizens of Rome, *everyone*.
(CHEERS.)
We expand, the demands grow daily, the claim on resources
is immense. Where next, you ask? Rome is the place we
make of it. No more or less. But it's no place now for the
belly-aching and fouling-up process of by-passing dogs—as
they must be passed by.
We believe, we have to, in ourselves, our children, our
Senate, with all its faults, *our* faults, *our* future. Our policies!
Our *Rome*! The rest will follow!
(*He stands down to an ovation—more or less—from the mob.
Stands waving and smiling at them. Enter* CAIUS MARCIUS
with escort.)
Welcome. Welcome to you, Caius Marcius.

VOICE: Welcome. Oh, yes, welcome, *Caius Marcius*!

MARCIUS (CORIOLANUS *from now*): Thanks. So what goes on here,
with these rabbling, purblind doomsters. Still scratching at
their opinions like armpits!

1ST CITIZEN: Not rhetoric! Already!

CORIOLANUS: What would you call this 'gathering' then? Noise
and ceasing to be yourselves. Do I hear laughter? Where
is it? No? It is a long time since I heard laughter any more
than a kind word among you.

1ST CITIZEN: You always have a kind word for *us*!

CORIOLANUS: You shouldn't lead with irony. It's not in your suit
and never will be. What is it they want, impoverished slobs.
Peace and war both intimidate you. You've no pride or fear

19

either. All you deserve or want is insult and good luck to the man who offers it to you. Whoever might deserve anything resembling greatness deserves your loathing. Good luck to him, I say. Nose pressing on windows and the stink and steam of your own breath and safe ways. God save the man who depends or waits on *your* wants. You don't believe me. You're capable of anything. Every minute some so-called mind changes itself. You cavil, haggle, you're wise after every event's been routed by the simplest of intuition. What's the matter with 'em? Almost anything they get 'd be too good for 'em. Now, what are they after?

MENENIUS: They've certain demands——

CORIOLANUS: Demands! What do they *offer*?

MENENIUS: They say——

CORIOLANUS: They say! Rot 'em.

VOICE: Rot *you!*

CORIOLANUS: No doubt. But it will be my choosing. They sit by the fire and—presume, presume to know. Know! What's done in the Capitol, who's on the way up or not, or down, think they can take sides and bring down their betters. They say! Demands! If everyone would lay aside this piety a moment, I'd soon have the heels of this mob.

MENENIUS: They do seem to have some idea of what they want. 'Searching critiques of the dominant ideas about politics and society', I think someone mentioned.

CORIOLANUS: Politics and society!

MENENIUS: Practice and theory.

CORIOLANUS: Practice and theory!

MENENIUS (*waffling in some confusion*): Industrial relations. Conformist ideals; technocratic skills, prevailing ideologies, vocational training, personnel management, investment planners.

CORIOLANUS: Prevailing ideologies.

MENENIUS: All phrases tend to get overheated in Rome.

CORIOLANUS: Well, they cool *my* blood. These shreds of personality have got enough already to break any generosity. *And* break the rule of law. Rather than obey if it's bad and get it changed. In a free and civilised Rome, this is all achieved not by

compulsion of authority but by the intelligence of individual
men. We still have our right to campaign for repeal or
amendment, and we've none of us believed otherwise.

VOICE: We!

CORIOLANUS: We! God grant I were ever *you!*

MENENIUS: What have we offered?

CORIOLANUS: Five tribunes of their own choice. One to be Junius
Brutus and the other Sicinius Velutus. Sicinius. And, oh and
God knows who else! God's death, they could have razed the
city before *I'd* agreed. Give them a mouldy metre and they'll
take the earth.

MENENIUS: It could lead all ways.

CORIOLANUS: Go get on to your homes, young marrieds, rising,
bright ones, citizens, (senior), ravers, scoffers, silent ones,
ones who speak their minds, turds, home, shower!
(*Enter a* MESSENGER *with briefcase and* ARMED GUARD.)

MESSENGER: Caius Marcius?

CORIOLANUS: Here. What is it?

MESSENGER: The Volscians are up in arms. And literally. A girl of
eight years old was murdered in the street an hour ago.

CORIOLANUS: Very well, then. Perhaps now we shall be seen to
have some use. But what does it matter. What is said, forecast,
commented on is what *matters*. Ah, senators, tribunes,
flowers of Rome.
(*Enter* SICINIUS VELUTUS, JUNIUS BRUTUS, COMINIUS, TITUS
LARTIUS *with* OTHER SENATORS. SICINIUS *is a pale-skinned
coloured woman.*)
Ah, Sicinius—a late entrance?

1ST SENATOR: Don't waste your spleen on Sicinius. The truth is
we are really and indeed at war with the Volscians now.

CORIOLANUS: Fancy. And what will Sicinius do about it? March
for them I've no doubt. But I tell you, they have a leader
already, Tullus Aufidius——

MOB: AU-FI-DI-US.

CORIOLANUS: Who might surprise you all. If I were not myself,
if I am even that, I would like nothing more than to be
Aufidius.

COMINIUS: You have fought——

CORIOLANUS: And will again, by the look of it.

1ST SENATOR: Then go with Cominius.

COMINIUS: You *did* pledge yourself——

CORIOLANUS: And why shouldn't I keep it? Titus Lartius, do you think you won't see me go in against Aufidius? What is it? Pressures is it? 'Comment' is it? Is it? What is the 'is'?

TITUS: No, no 'is', Caius Marcius. I have made my position clear, I think.

CORIOLANUS: Well done!

MENENIUS: Yes, well said.

1ST SENATOR: Let's go to the Capitol, most of 'em are behind us.

TITUS (*to* COMINIUS): Let's go. (*to* CORIOLANUS) Give your support to Cominius. To us you are something more than an elected deputy.

CORIOLANUS: What deputy ever became leader?

COMINIUS: Dear Marcius, your place is assured and your recognition *will* come.
(*He raises his hand.*)

1ST SENATOR (*to* Roman CITIZENS): Get off home, to your families, your workbenches, both sides of industries, your floors, we shall all sit down.

CORIOLANUS: And get piles or paunches or the both. You've done well today; led from behind and observed from the front. Get the feel of them.
(*He, the* SENATORS *and the* MOB *leave in an uproar of banner waving, shouting, singing, journalists weaving, cameras wobbling, some waving to the audience they are performing to. Leaving the two tribunes alone.*)

SICINIUS: Was there anyone ever as arrogant or obvious as Marcius?

BRUTUS: No one.

SICINIUS: When we were chosen as tribunes for the people——

BRUTUS: Did you see his expression?

SICINIUS: See it! Hear it!

BRUTUS: Don't be deceived. When he's moved, which is too much of the time, he will go for anything or anyone, and someone will always be there to listen to him.

SICINIUS: Or record it. But there's a coldness.

BRUTUS: That's right. That's his strength.

SICINIUS: He'll be eaten soon enough. He's got too much conceit
in him as it is. Can you see him being bum boy to Cominius?
BRUTUS: Cominius is a decrepit bully boy general grown old.
He'll be blamed for being too old, if there's any blame. And
if there's any triumph going, Marcius will have the edge on
him.
SICINIUS: Besides, Caius Marcius might lose, but, in these days of
fashion and upstarts, Caius Marcius is the man to watch.
BRUTUS: He'll be watched all right. Let's go.
COMINIUS: Let's.

SCENE THREE

CORIOLI. *The Senate House. Enter* TULLUS AUFIDIUS *with* SENATORS.

1ST SENATOR: So, Aufidius, think Rome knows every which
way what's going on here?
AUFIDIUS: Don't you? Everything here or, indeed, anywhere, is
known almost before it's happened. I first heard—I think
I've got the letter here. Yes. Here it is. They've troopments
at the ready. Cominius; Marcius, *your* old enemy. They hate
in Rome as much as here if not more so. Titus Lartius,
thought a 'good sort'. These three: not bad leaders. Think
on it.
1ST SENATOR: Our army's ready. We never doubted Rome would
ever be any different.
AUFIDIUS: We could have taken every town before Rome had
woken up to it.
2ND SENATOR: Bring your army up, Aufidius; but, knowing them,
I think you'll find they're still not ready for us.
AUFIDIUS: Not ready? Oh, I'm only talking of certainties and one
of those if ever there was one is Caius Marcius. If he and
I could just ever *meet*—neither of us can do any more—till
that time.

SCENE FOUR

Rome. A room in CORIOLANUS'S *house.* VOLUMNIA, *his mother and* VIRGILIA, *his wife.*

VOLUMNIA: What a glum mood you're in. If I had my son for a husband I should hope I'd put a better face on it, than you are; considering what he's at. I remember when he was very tiny, he seemed the only thing life would ever yield up to me; I wouldn't let him a wink out of sight. Even so, I don't think I ever held him back the once; always *forward*— at least that's what I tried to do, and now it's no more different than all those other times; oh, long before he became what he is since. Didn't I let him go to a violent, rotten and filthy war? And didn't he come back practically weighed down with citations and awards like he did when he was a schoolboy? I tell you, Virgilia, I am more proud at this moment, if it's possible, than the first time I set eyes on him.

VIRGILIA: Supposing he had fallen back—even a little? Let alone died in all this thrusting and ambition?

VOLUMNIA: 'Thrusting and ambition' you call it! Its very existence was reputation enough for me. If I had a dozen sons and I loved every one of them as much as my- and your-Marcius, I'd rather the whole lot of them snuffed out and for a good cause than one of them come up to Marcius's scratch.
(*Enter* SERVANT)

SERVANT: Madam, Lady Valeria is here.

VIRGILIA: Forgive me but I'll go.

VOLUMNIA: Indeed you won't. Oh, I see, your husband's gesture; his voice in the air; seeing what he'll *do* to someone like Aufidius. Do you really think he has a chance against such a man, a *man*, a man like ours? I can hear him say 'Come on, you lot. You were all begotten in timidity even if you'd been born in Rome. There's no blood in you. Red piss.'

VIRGILIA: Red piss, as you call it's bad enough to watch without more blood.

VOLUMNIA: You cowish little idiot. What do you know about blood?
(to SERVANT) Well, don't keep Lady Valeria waiting.
(to VIRGILIA) We've got lots to chat about.

VIRGILIA: All I can say is, or think is, God save my husband
from Aufidius, or indeed anyone like him.

VOLUMNIA: Aufidius! He'd beat him into the ground.

(*Enter* VALERIA.)

VALERIA: Well, hallo.

VOLUMNIA: My dear Valeria.

VIRGILIA: How nice to see you.

VALERIA: But how are you both? Aren't these terrible times?
I mean they're just terrible. What are you doing there
decorating? But it looks perfectly splendid. And how's
the little son, the little grandchild?

VIRGILIA: He's well enough for his age. Thanks to his grand-
mother's looking after.

VOLUMNIA: I know my grandson. He'd rather be up and about
and doing things. One day. Changing things. Worthwhile
things. Than moping about the state of things at home.

VALERIA: His father's son all right. And so pretty as well. Do
you know, I looked at him last Wednesday for a whole
half an hour—that face, that *determination*, what do you call
it, resolve. I saw him chase a butterfly in your garden here,
and do you know, he wouldn't even let *that* little creature
baulk him! I don't know whether it was his falling down and
knees all scratched and bruised, but he was in such a rage,
that child, in such a *torrent*, nothing could have saved that
doomed insect.

VOLUMNIA: Just like his father.

VALERIA: Wouldn't give an inch.

VIRGILIA: Not an inch . . .

VALERIA: Come along. Let's have some fun together in your
lovely garden.

VIRGILIA: I'm not going out of doors.

VALERIA: Not going out of doors?

VOLUMNIA: Oh, she will, you see.

VIRGILIA: No, if you'll forgive me, I won't. I'm not moving from
this house; not even into that garden until His Lordship's
come back from all his rhetoricizing and legalized brawlings.

VALERIA: Come, you musn't upset yourself. There's lots to do
while he's away.

25

VIRGILIA: It's not that I'm lazy, as you think, or busy as *I* think.

VALERIA: Can't waste time; especially now.

VIRGILIA: I'd rather it used *me* rather than busy my*self*.

VALERIA: Honestly, go along with me because I really do have the most exciting news for you; yes, your husband.

VIRGILIA: There can't be any yet.

VALERIA: No, honestly, I tell you. I heard it last night.

VIRGILIA: What did you hear then?

VALERIA: Well, aren't I telling you? I heard it from a Senator. Simply this: the Volscians have raised an enormous army. General Cominius has taken some battalions or whatever they're called from the Roman Army and, guess who's immediately behind it, but Titus Lartius and your very own husband. By this time they must be fanned out; is that what they call it? Anyway, entrenched or something, in strategic positions or something, right in front of Corioli itself. And from all accounts, they don't mean to stay *there* long. They'll deal with them soon enough, you can take it from me. It's true, I promise you. So come along, you should be pleased.

VIRGILIA: Forgive me, Valeria, I've not yet taken this in.

VOLUMNIA: Oh, leave her alone, Valeria, whatever news you tell her she'll do nothing but mope and be a misery.

VALERIA: I'm beginning to think you're right. Well, see you later. Oh, come along, Virgilia, give yourself a face-lift and forget the war for an afternoon. The dreariness of the winter and strikes and dark evenings.

VIRGILIA: In a word, no. I will not and I must not, so both go and enjoy yourselves.

VALERIA: Please yourself—of course.

(VOLUMNIA *and* VALERIA *leave* VIRGILIA *to herself.*)

SCENE FIVE

Oblique, battle-torn area on the outskirts of Corioli. Enter SOLDIERS *with* CORIOLANUS *and* TITUS LARTIUS. *Flak jackets, berets, helmets, rifles, shields, home-made bombs and bottles hurling, the sound of gunfire and sniping, etc. From the flies a parachute descends bearing a heavily armed* PARATROOPER. *Before this,* CORIOLANUS *has been observing his descent keenly through binoculars.*

CORIOLANUS (*to* LARTIUS): A fiver they've made contact.

LARTIUS: Ten.

CORIOLANUS: Done.

LARTIUS: Right.

(*The* PARATROOPER *lands with a clang of boots and rubble and is helped out of his parachute. He approaches* CORIOLANUS *and salutes smartly.*)

CORIOLANUS: Well, have they made contact?

PARATROOPER: They're giving each other's eyeballs a good going over, sir, but no action as such yet.

LARTIUS: Well, that's a tenner up your spout.

CORIOLANUS: How far away?

PARATROOPER: Mile and a half.

CORIOLANUS: Right, this'll be it soon enough. With God's good luck, we should blow the bleeding bejesus out of them in five minutes and back up those poor sods being shot at out there for damn all. What do you say, Lartius?

LARTIUS: Let's get to it.

(*The* ROMAN SOLDIERS *prepare to advance in splendid regimental style, poised on the edge of streets, and so on, when* TWO SOLDIERS *of Corioli appear in para-military uniform and nonchalantly waving white flags.*)

CORIOLANUS: So, there you are. Tell me, Tullus Aufidius, is he still stuck behind your barricades?

IST SOLDIER: No, and there's not one of us that's less afraid of you than he is.

CORIOLANUS: What a strange race they are. All verbal quirks and long top lips.

(*Sound of drums and sniping.*)

IST SOLDIER: D'ye hear that then? That's our lads alright. We'll rip down our barricades rather than see you pound us up like dogs but we'll do it when it suits us.

(*More noise of rifle fire off stage.*)

D'ye hear that then? How far away d'ye think that is?

And who do you think it is? That's Aufidius, that is.
D'ye hear what he's doing to your poor under-paid
professionals?
LARTIUS: Get back before someone kills you. Right, lads.
(*The* SOLDIERS *retreat, jeering and throwing stones as the*
ROMAN SOLDIERS *prepare to stand ground.*)
CORIOLANUS: They don't look afraid, but if they don't, it's because
of no imagination; and without imagination, take it from
me, you won't find much skill, just random wind. You
know your equipment, you know how to use it and to use it
well; and to use your brains, which is a damn sight more
useful than anything they've got to pitch againt us, or ever
shall have. Let's get in there, Titus—why do we let them
waste our time with chat and drums and banners. Anyone
who holds back, he'll deal with me and forget he ever heard
the word regulations.
(*The* ROMANS *charge down the street with a terrifying noise.*
For a while, all we hear is the sound of automatic rifles, shouting
and so on. After some of this, they are beaten back to behind
their coils of barbed wire, armoured vehicles, etc., led by
CORIOLANUS.)
CORIOLANUS: Call yourselves bloody Romans! May the world's
pox rot your bollocks off. Let you all stew in the pus of your
sisters' cunts so you stink a mile off. You little goosey-
gander men, what are you *doing*; running from red bog faced
layabouts that my six-year-old'd stand up to. Balls of fire!
What is this—a whole company without a mark except those
shot up the arse! Now hear me! Get those miserable faces
turned round the right way and get stuck into it or as sure
as God made little apples, and you rotten lot, I'll turn round
and I'll start my own private war with you—and make no
mistake who'd win. Come on then! Get your fingers out and-
we'll-be in-crumpet-before-them!
(*A gap appears in the barricade at the other end of the street.*)
There's an opening! Get in there! And if it isn't your
birthday, you weren't *born*.
(CORIOLANUS *dashes through the opening and disappears.*)
IST SOLDIER: It's not my birthday.

2ND SOLDIER: Mine neither. Haven't been born long *enough*,
    anyway.
1ST SOLDIER: Look, they've really got him in this time.
    (*Noise and gunfire off from the direction of the closed barricade.*)
2ND SOLDIER: Short and curly's department this time, I'll bet.
    (*Enter* TITUS LARTIUS.)
LARTIUS: Where's your commander?
1ST SOLDIER: Halted at the barricades looks like, sir. Right behind
    them he was before you could say how's your father.
    Next thing he's disappeared. All on his tod. Dressed up and
    nowhere else to go but *in*.
LARTIUS: Oh, Marcius, only you. No-one else.
1ST SOLDIER: Dead right, sir.
2ND SOLDIER: Looks like that's it, then.
1ST SOLDIER: Look, sir.
    (*Enter* CORIOLANUS, *having forced himself back through the
    barricade obviously seriously wounded and covered in blood.
    He beckons wildly to* LARTIUS.)
LARTIUS: Well, don't gape at the poor bastard—follow up!
    (*A slight pause and the* ROMANS *follow* LARTIUS *and bearing*
    CORIOLANUS *with them, disappear behind the barricades.*)

SCENE SIX

Inside Corioli.
Enter TWO ROMAN SOLDIERS *under fire and stone throwing.*

1ST SOLDIER: Don't fancy that lot.
2ND SOLDIER: As Caius Marcius says, they're not a lovable lot.
1ST SOLDIER: I don't want love, I just want out of this ugly
    bleeding army. Watch it.
    (*They duck from a sniper's volley.* CORIOLANUS *and* TITUS LARTIUS
    enter. The first contemplates TITUS, *very much on his guard.*)
CORIOLANUS: There's a certain sound about ammunition wasting
    itself. The ill-trained warlike wanker. How do you think our
    lads have made out?
TITUS: On the whole, they've held. As you well know, Caius, if

they make mistakes their orders sometimes actually require it. Allowance has to be made for the situations of war, call it what you like. We can't guarantee or legislate against painful or hasty headed decisions, any more than wisdom as well as bravery and initiative.

CORIOLANUS: Aufidius is the man. If we can get *him!* Titus, take what you think you need to mop up the city. What's left I'll take with me to back up Cominius.

TITUS: You're wounded. Orderly!

CORIOLANUS: I'm not even wound up yet. A bit of blood letting's good for the likes of me so long as it doesn't weaken the natural spleen too much when I catch up with friend Aufidius. Just so long as he recognises me.

TITUS: He will!

(*Exit* CORIOLANUS.)

(*to* RADIO SIGNALLER): Get all officers you can contact and we'll meet in the old market. If it's still there. Get on with it. (*He rushes off.*)

(*The* SIGNALLER *disappears into his armoured vehicle. Enter* COMINIUS, *looking grim, with* SOLDIERS *in support.*)

COMINIUS: Take a breather, lads. You did well; like people'll have learned to expect from Roman troops in spite of what they say. Sensible and restrained under fire; and calm and disciplined in retreat. Rest while you get the chance. They won't leave us for long.

(*The* SIGNALLER *puts his head out of the radio van.*)

Well? Got anything?

SIGNALLER: Seems like Lartius and Marcius got caught in a frontal assault from half Corioli. There's a running battle. But I think Marcius is trying to limit the area.

COMINIUS: Keep contact.

(*Enter* CORIOLANUS.)

CORIOLANUS: Am I too late?

COMINIUS: Not while you are here.

CORIOLANUS: Old devil!

(*They clasp hands.*)

COMINIUS: As usual. Giving them shit where it's needed, which is everywhere, then belting on. And the men?

CORIOLANUS: All right without their tribunes to make them down
warfare for shorter hours, thank you. They're well paid to
be shot at. If you can be well *paid*. It's difficult to know
which side the fire came from. But why are you back here?
COMINIUS: We weren't doing so well. I think I followed the
what-ye-call-it battle concept as we went over it.
CORIOLANUS: Move, move, move! Yes . . . The orders were clear.
Where do they seem concentrated? With Aufidius?
COMINIUS: Who else?
CORIOLANUS: Let me go back.
COMINIUS: You're in no proper state. Still, I can't say no. Take
what you need with you.
CORIOLANUS: Volunteers. And volunteers I *do* mean. The rest can
stay behind, those who come for the uniform, the ride, and
all the rest of it.
(*They all yell enthusiastically.*)
Well done! But for Aufidius, we need not just the best but
the fastest. The rest had better stay here with Cominius.
COMINIUS: Do as he says. Take your pick.
CORIOLANUS: You, you, you, you, (*etc.*)
COMINIUS: Let's go.
(*They divide and disappear. Enter* TITUS LARTIUS *with* ROMAN
TROOPS.)
TITUS: Keep these barricades. If we abandon the outskirts, we'll
get holed up inside.
SOLDIER: Yes, sir.
TITUS: Watch and try to make contact. Come on.
(*Goes with the rest. Quiet. Then* CORIOLANUS *and* AUFIDIUS *are
seen to be stalking each other with rifles and/or pistols through
street windows and doors and crouching behind rubble and oil
cans.*)
CORIOLANUS (*shouts*): I'll have you, Aufidius. You're the one.
AUFIDIUS: And you're mine.
CORIOLANUS: Let's have you.
AUFIDIUS: Let's see you run.
CORIOLANUS: I? RUN! You'd better do better than you're doing
now.
AUFIDIUS: Got you.

(Rapid exchange of fire between them, desparate running and dodging as each almost kills the other. Some VOLSCIANS *come to their Leader's aid.)*

CORIOLANUS: Reinforcements crawling up, eh, you slum rat! Vermin always need other vermin! See you.

(He disappears under a volley of fire from AUFIDIUS, *who curses to his followers, then also disappears. After a while a badly wounded* CORIOLANUS *is led in by* COMINIUS *and troops.)*

COMINIUS: Thank God for you, Caius.

(Enter TITUS.*)*

TITUS: Have you seen!

CORIOLANUS: Berserk. We've done what we could.

COMINIUS: Rome will know about it and judge for themselves. They always do. And they shall know the truth of it, not some seeking, rabbling accounts of it from outsiders.

CORIOLANUS *(in pain)*: Ah.

(Two ORDERLIES *attend on him. There are a few cheers.)*
Wait for the reports, the courts, the writers after the events; the ones who'll call *us* bloody and never mind your wounds or skill or patience. They won't tell you then your Roman's better than any other in the world, spat at, abused, cheerful and always shot at. And in their favourite target—the back.

COMINIUS: Be thankful for small tributes. But they won't be small; we'll see to that. Rome shall know.

ALL: Lord Coriolanus!

COMINIUS: Aye, and no joke either. Caius Marcius; Lord Coriolanus.

ALL: Caius Marcius, CORIOLANUS!

(CHEERS.)

COMINIUS: Rome shall know. I promise you. Titus, set up your headquarters.

CORIOLANUS: Can I just do one thing. An old woman in the street down there—and then I saw Aufidius.

COMINIUS: We'll see to it. Which house?

CORIOLANUS: Ye Gods, I've forgotten! I'm tired suddenly. Is there a drink?

COMINIUS: Let's go in there. That looks nasty. Sergeant!

(ORDERLIES bear off CORIOLANUS. *The rest follow.)*

SCENE SEVEN

The camp of the VOLSCIANS. *An old hall with trestle tables, maps, flags, guns, bombs, ammunition. Enter* AUFIDIUS, *bloodstained, with followers.*

AUFIDIUS: Well, the town's taken.

1ST LIEUTENANT: We'll get it back on the right terms.

AUFIDIUS: Terms. I wish I were a Roman at this moment—almost. Terms! What terms can be right that *we* don't make. Five times I've fought against you, Marcius, and always I'm made a meal of. God, if we ever meet again, it's his eyeballs or mine. I'll have him all to myself the next time.

1ST LIEUTENANT: He's the devil all right.

AUFIDIUS: Just as bold if not quite so subtle. Nothing, not sleep, food, religion, esteem, Capitol; nor all the interests of intercedence or arbitration come between me and my Marcius. If I find him, in bed with his wife or tied to his child and mother, I'll have that heart out and any going with it . . . Go into the city. Find out what's happening, hostages, help from outside, any report you can get, any source.

1ST LIEUTENANT: Won't you come?

AUFIDIUS: They're waiting for me at our arranged point across the border. Get to it and find out so that I can get on accordingly.

1ST LIEUTENANT: Sir!
(Salutes stiffly and goes out, leaving AUFIDIUS *brooding in the dust and darkness of his trestle table and blackboards.)*

SCENE EIGHT

Rome. A conference room. Informal. MENENIUS *is talking conversationally with* TRIBUNES *of the people,* SICINIUS *and* BRUTUS.

MENENIUS: Well, the indications are, gentlemen, that there will be news before the night is out.

BRUTUS: Good or bad?

MENENIUS: If I am informed correctly, not what your so-called

man in the street will welcome very much; knowing as we
do how they feel about Marcius.

SICINIUS: Simplest of animals, lambs, to know at once who likes
you or not.

MENENIUS: Tell me then, who would you say the wolf loves?

SICINIUS: The lamb.

MENENIUS: Yes, to destroy him. After using him. Like the Plebians
would do to Marcius given the merest chance.

BRUTUS: He's a lamb all right. Unfortunately he makes noises
more like a bear.

MENENIUS: He may make the noises of a bear to you and me but
within the fugitive place that strange sound comes from
I assure you, gentlemen, there is quite the smallest of lambs.
Tell me one thing. You are both up with the times and know
all that's going on. Tell me something that seems to escape
me at the moment.

SICINIUS: Well?

MENENIUS: What fault do you think it is; that it is; that Marcius
has that you two may not have even more of?

BRUTUS: I can't think of any he hasn't inherited—like most of
his kind; and looked after well and brought to every dividend
you can think of.

SICINIUS: Pride's gilt-edged.

BRUTUS: Some modest trading in old-fashioned Roman boasting
is always good for a bit.

MENENIUS: How very interesting. Having said that, what would
you say was the opinion of you here in the city—I mean
all those of us you'd call 'the other side'? Do you know
or does it never bother you, I suppose.

SICINIUS: So what is *their* opinion?

MENENIUS: Only that—you understand we are talking of pride
now—so you won't be angry.

SICINIUS: Why should we?

MENENIUS: Why should you? I can think of very little that could
ever make you climb down or change your sides, but
as we are just together, the three of us, tell me what
it is you really think; and it'll go no further. Now: you blame
Marcius for the sin of pride.

BRUTUS: We are not exactly alone in that.

MENENIUS: Oh, I know you would not feel it if you were in any way alone. You have too much on your side, perhaps the course of history itself. Otherwise you might appear some time to be no more than just ingenuous eccentrics or something of the kind. Your talents are too blessedly childlike to be used anywhere but inside oh, what; play-groups and working crowds. You talk of pride; if you could only just once, the once, look inwards and make a good old inner survey of your own good selves; see what lies among the old props holding up the faces of those worked-on seams; that I would like to see very much.

SICINIUS: Would you, and what *then*?

MENENIUS: I think that you might discover a pair of the most unmeriting, proud, over-exposed, vicious and violent middle men and (to SICINIUS) sorry—women, we have ever had or known in Rome.

SICINIUS: Menenius, let me tell you, let me tell you and you surely must know it, that everyone knows well enough what you are and have done for a long time.

MENENIUS: Indeed I do. I have a reputation for wit and every irony which as we all know, is always disastrous for a politician. Also that I like good food and wine and don't prefer the muck in the market place without questioning, merely because it is the most known and the most available. On the other hand, when I do believe in what I say, my malice is wasted as much as any one else's. No-one believes in that either. If I sit down with two statesmen like yourself, I cannot take you seriously any more than you me. When you give me your beer or tea to drink, it just isn't in me to pretend I like the stuff.

SICINIUS: Which is why you love Marcius?

MENENIUS: Which is *one* reason why I love Caius Marcius. I can't say that you impress me either with your arguments or the delivery of them; I have to appear to go along with those who say that you are serious and clever. I can only say that I don't like the look of either of you. Even I am a better sight to look on than either of you two; but I am sure you would be the first to agree that this is very inconsequential. Tell me what it is that you see in me; what is it that's so bad; so calculating, so insignificant; so resolutely turned against Rome's future; and only of benefit to my own ends?

BRUTUS: Come, sir, we know you.

MENENIUS: You don't know me, yourselves, or any other damn thing. Oh, you are all out for standing ovations and outstretched hands. You'll spend a sunny morning on the same sides of the table arguing the case between two pins and one and come back happily in the afternoon; when it happens to suit you, you'll put on any kind of act providing that you think it'll *work*. Start roaring out for marches, demonstrations in the streets and barricades and bloody flags and who knows what. All the messiahs of your own voices. The only peace you ever make is abusing everyone. Oh yes, my friends, you are a pair of strange ones.

BRUTUS: Come, come, Menenius. You know, and we know, that you'll be better remembered as an after dinner speaker in the provinces rather than a serious politician in the Capitol.

MENENIUS: Even priests have to mock sometimes when they're confronted with the truly insignificant absurd. Well, I suppose you must be saying, still saying, that Marcius is proud; who at the merest calculation is worth more than you and all your predecessors since I can bother to remember. Perhaps the best of them might have inherited the skills of an executioner and that's about the lot. Good night, my friends. More of your conversation at this time of night would honestly make my brain reel; like a shepherd with a lot of drunken sheep to round up. I hope I haven't been too open. I don't *think* I have.

(*He gets up and leaves* BRUTUS *and* SICINIUS *alone in their chairs.*)

SICINIUS: People like him are only open behind closed doors.

(BRUTUS *takes out a sheet of paper and hands it to* SICINIUS.)

BRUTUS: Caius Marcius is coming home.

SICINIUS: I see. He'll have more cause than ever to strut about.

SCENE NINE

Airport near Rome. MENENIUS, ATTENDANTS, POLICEMEN, *etc. Enter* VOLUMNIA, VIRGILIA *and* VALERIA.

VOLUMNIA: Menenius, my dear, good friend. Marcius, my boy Marcius is on his way. He's coming home.

MENENIUS: Almost here. (*He looks up*)

VOLUMNIA: And, Menenius, look at the crowds here to greet him, all along the route from Rome, as well as here!

MENENIUS: I know. And thank heaven for them. (*He embraces* VOLUMNIA) Hooray. Marcius coming home.

VOLUMNIA: Look, here's a letter from him! The State's got another, his wife another; and, oh, I think there's one at home for you.

MENENIUS: At my house. Those fools must have made me miss it. I'll dash home after, make no mistake. I feel a new man, already. He is the best cure there is for any of us. Aches, pains or what you will. Is he well?

VIRGILIA: Oh, no, no, no.

VOLUMNIA: If he isn't, we'll take care of him and thank heavens we can.

MENENIUS: If it's not too bad this time.

VOLUMNIA: This is the third time he has come home to all this.

MENENIUS: I understand he salted Aufidius's tail for him.

VOLUMNIA: Titus Lartius says they got barrel to barrel but Aufidius got off.

MENENIUS: Not too soon, I'll bet. We must see that a full statement is made to the Senate before any questioning in the middle of all this.

VOLUMNIA: Let's look out for him. Yes, yes, yes. The Senate has had the General's report *and* my son's part in it.

VALERIA: Isn't it exciting! Where can we see best?

MENENIUS: Exciting! Yes, and well-sweated for.

VIRGILIA: If only it all goes well.

VOLUMNIA: Well? How else *can* it.

MENENIUS (*to the* TRIBUNES, *who have appeared*): Just in time, my good friends. He's almost here. Where is he wounded?

VOLUMNIA: All over. They'll see.

VIRGILIA (*looking up at the sky*): Not if I can help it.

VALERIA: One in the neck and two in the thigh I was told——

VOLUMNIA: Twenty-five before he ever started this campaign.

MENENIUS: Here he comes.

VIRGILIA: Where! Where!

MENENIUS: Just listen to that noise.

VIRGILIA: Damn the noise. Where is he?

VOLUMNIA: The cause of all this?

(*The airport has gone wild with shouting and chanting.*)

VIRGILIA: And the tears he's left behind him.

VOLUMNIA: Not Marcius. *They* brought their deaths on them*selves*.
He's the arm, if you like, not all of it, mind.

VIRGILIA: Nor heart, I should hope.

(*Shouts and some confusion.* COMINIUS *and* TITUS LARTIUS
enter. Between them, discreetly but dashingly uniformed, is
CORIOLANUS, *accompanied by* MEDICAL ORDERLIES, OFFICIALS,
etc. Shouts of 'Caius Marcius', 'Lord Marcius of Corioli,'
'Corio-lan-us! Corio-lan-us!')

CORIOLANUS: Are they all gone mad or what? That will do, I think.
I've seen enough sickening things today; even for my stomach.

COMINIUS: Your mother's here.

CORIOLANUS: Oh, I know you're all overjoyed——

VOLUMNIA: Don't be modest, of all things; my by-rights-gentle
Marcius; Caius who always truly 'deserved'. And now you
receive it; however brief it may turn out to be, however
much of a one night stand; it's yours, and yours by your own
efforts. But, Caius, no, what is it we must call you now?
Oh, here's your wife. Now the Lady——

CORIOLANUS: I've seen and done bad things.

MENENIUS: No, no. You are tired, you need rest; make some
space there!

CORIOLANUS: Valeria, my dear, forgive me.

VOLUMNIA: I don't know what to say. Cominius, welcome back,
all of you.

MENENIUS: Yes, all of you. It's a sad day and a good, for all that.
Anyone here will see that.

COMINIUS: Quite so. Make way along there. Make a path.

CORIOLANUS (*to* VOLUMNIA *and* VIRGILIA): Here! Both of you.
  Before I ever get home there are people I've got to see.
  Of course. It just has to be done.
VOLUMNIA: Today, everything I have ever wanted is true; yours
  and mine; so what can anything else matter? There is only
  one thing left for Rome to offer you and, after this, I can't
  see them refusing it you.
CORIOLANUS: You have an instinct in these things, matters, Mother.
COMINIUS: Time for us to get off to the Capitol.
  (*In some confusion and clamour, as before, they go, leaving*
  SICINIUS *and* BRUTUS.)
BRUTUS: For a few hours, he'll be different to the rest of us.
  Apparently. Until it turns out, is made out, different.
SICINIUS: Just as you say. But with such supporters, who needs——
BRUTUS: Enemies . . . True.
SICINIUS: People in Rome don't forget their fathers and
  grandfathers on account of one day's bit of circus. They're
  familiar enough with all this bit. They're just as quick to be
  antagonized.
BRUTUS: I've heard him say enough times, and you too, that he'll
  never 'put himself up to the mob'—quick though he is to
  use 'em when it suits him. *I* can't see him putting himself
  up to please. Can you? Unless appearing, mark, *appearing*
  to displease, when the wind's in the right place and then only
  then.
SICINIUS: Right, Then let's make sure of it.
BRUTUS: That everyone is quite certain in their own minds what
  he really means and thinks of them.
SICINIUS: He will. They will know. He'll see to that. The rest is
  up to us.
  (*Enter a* MESSENGER.)
  What is it?
MESSENGER: You're to go to the Capitol. Marcius is up for Consul
  already. The returns are overwhelmingly in his favour.
  I'm astonished you're not there.
SICINIUS: We know. You forget. We have been there before.
  (*They go out.*)

SCENE TEN

Rome. A public place. Outcry. TWO SENIOR POLICE OFFICERS *conduct the crowd and observe.*

2ND POLICE OFFICER: They all say Coriolanus will have his way, in spite of all this.

1ST POLICE OFFICER: Oh, he's brave enough and clever enough. But *is* he clever enough—he loves no-one here today, that's for sure. If any day. And shows it what's more.

2ND POLICE OFFICER: There have been plenty enough in the past to govern the people without *liking* them; let alone loving them. They've flattered without even hating them, like Coriolanus does.

1ST POLICE OFFICER: No one can hate so spectacularly without being tied up by love somewhere.

2ND POLICE OFFICER: Who knows? It'll end soon enough. In the meantime, we've enough on *our* hands to see that he gets a safe escort while he's with us to still need it.
(*Enter the* PATRICIANS, *and the* TRIBUNES *of the people; they are moving forward and are just held back as* CORIOLANUS, MENENIUS *and* COMINIUS—*now dressed as a Consul*—*enter.* SICINIUS *and* BRUTUS *separate themselves and take up prominent positions by the people of Rome.*)

MENENIUS (*silencing the crowd, more or less*): Having done with— yes, done with I say, done with the Volsces, and apart from recalling Titus Lartius, the main business, the only truly pleasurable one in all this business, it should be publicly spelled out what part was played in the very best of that tragic business by: Caius Marcius Coriolanus.

SOME CRIES OF: CORIO-LAN-US!

MENENIUS: Which is why we are rallied here together; all sections and representatives of the people of Rome; patricians, so-called plebians, tribunes of the people, consuls, we are all, yes, all I say, *citizens of Rome*. And who is not proud to say so?

SICINIUS: Let's hear from Coriolanus himself on that.

1ST SENATOR: You speak first, Cominius. Leave nothing out.

(*to the* TRIBUNES) Let him have the floor, and then it will be your turn.

SICINIUS: We are here to listen as well as say our piece. Always have been.

BRUTUS: We can't always be expected though to control carefully calculated incitements to the ordinary people; the Heart of Rome itself. That's *your* time-honoured occupation; indeed, obsession.

MENENIUS: That's not on. Not on at all. I'd rather you'd not said that. On second thoughts——

SICINIUS: As always——

MENENIUS: I'm glad you did. Will you allow Cominius to speak?

BRUTUS: Certainly. I was merely pointing out that you cannot blame us for not having the resources to control situations created by yourselves.

MENENIUS: He has never had anything but the love of his country and of you all as his first thought. Tell 'em, Cominius.
(CORIOLANUS *rises and offers to go away*.)

MENENIUS: No, stay where you are.

CORIOLANUS: Please to forgive me. I'd rather go back to it all than hear it gone over and how it came about.

BRUTUS: Sir, I hope nothing we've said has upset your stomach for these very typical Roman occasions. Every voice must let itself be heard.

CORIOLANUS: *Heard!* You call slogans and horses charged by your waving banners, being heard! I've got as much stomach for all of that as——

MENENIUS: Sit down!

CORIOLANUS: I'd rather sit at home and think; picking my cat's fleas for him than go in for whatever you call this—making speeches about what I may or may not have done . . .
(*Exit* CORIOLANUS.)

MENENIUS: Cominius!
(*Some boos and cat calls follow* CORIOLANUS.)

COMINIUS: Now, now——

VOICE: Speak up!

COMINIUS: I am here. What can I say of one man? When all you understand is parties, factions, invented plots, insights,

misbegotten, slavering, from the inside reports. You talk of
pride, some of you. It *is* one part of that man. I couldn't be
that man, but I wish that one of you could even be a little
less than one part of that man. His flaws are lasting
monuments already, while your well-planned assessments
and schemes and developments are brought into this world
like the bright, deformed slums they were always; conceived
in clever ignorance. He doesn't want anything——

SICINIUS: He's got it already——

COMINIUS: What he was born with . . .

MENENIUS: Call him back. Call Coriolanus back.

(*Dissension and indecision in the crowd.*)

2ND POLICE OFFICER: Here he is, sir.

(*Enter* CORIOLANUS.)

MENENIUS: The Senate, Coriolanus, *will* be pleased to make you
consul.

CORIOLANUS: As you wish.

MENENIUS: The only thing left is to make your platform
acceptable all round.

CORIOLANUS: Please, I do ask you not even to try to do that. I
can't play kiss my arse and ask for favours or votes of
confidence. Not even to make them feel the illusion of
power, or the ritual bestowings of it. Please, let me out of
this one.

SICINIUS: Sir, you must speak to the people; the people of Rome.
Speak yourself to them, that's all they ask of you.

CORIOLANUS: Must I? Must I? Then I think it's time I must *not*.

SICINIUS: They have a right at least to all the forms.

MENENIUS: Do as they say. We all have to do it.

CORIOLANUS: 'Having to'. 'Forms' may not necessarily be 'rights'.

BRUTUS (*to* SICINIUS): You hear that.

CORIOLANUS: To *have* to say I did this for you and then that.
What I had to for them without pain to myself.

MENENIUS: Don't make an issue of this. It's everyday coinage—
or conversion, change over; redevelopment; re-thinking;
streamlining; adjusting to new needs, circumstances—you
know the phrases.

CORIOLANUS: I do. I am not obliged to *use* them.

MENENIUS: You are, my friend, or you will be. Tribunes of the People, you see our choice.

SICINIUS: We do.

SENATORS: CORIO-LAN-US!

(*They go out, leaving* TRIBUNES *and* STRAGGLERS. *Band plays.* CROWD *starts to break up.*)

BRUTUS: You see where his mind's going?

SICINIUS: Do you think we are the only ones? He will have to put his case to them; *and* tout around for seals of approval from all kinds of places he affects to detest.

BRUTUS: Come. We've got a campaign of our own to work out.

SCENE ELEVEN

Rome. A public place near the forum. An election van with hailer on top and CORIOLANUS *posters. Enter several* CITIZENS.

1ST CITIZEN: If he's not so stubborn and can bring himself to listen as well as talk, and talk *to* us, I don't see why he shouldn't have our votes.

2ND CITIZEN: That's for all of us to make up our minds.

3RD CITIZEN: I'd say we could do worse.

(*Enter* CORIOLANUS, *unobtrusively dressed, rather like the* CITIZENS, *with* MENENIUS.)

There he is, looking like any man in the street. Let's split up and go up to him in ones and twos—on the quiet. Everyone can put a question to him about his own problems. That way he can't complain of facing an incoherent, unreasoning or unlistening mob.

MENENIUS: My dear chap, we've all had to do it in the past, not only now; the greatest men in Rome have cheerfully subjected themselves to it.

CORIOLANUS: 'Cheerfully subjected'. What do I say to them? It makes my tongue all ulcerated to think of myself.

MENENIUS: Do not think of your*self*; and don't abuse your tongue or you'll end up with even more than ulcers in your hands.

Think of Rome—of Rome alone. You need its popular
support—to begin with—not just the respect of a few of us.

CORIOLANUS: Popular support. I'd rather be forgotten by them all.

MENENIUS: You'll ruin everything. Think about it. Try speaking
to them in an ordinary, friendly way.

(*Goes out.*)

CORIOLANUS: No such thing.

(*Three* CITIZENS *approach.*)

Tell them I hope they've had their weekly bath and cleaned
their teeth. Ah, here's a couple . . . You know why I'm
standing about here?

3RD CITIZEN: We do, sir. Some call it the 'hustings'.

CORIOLANUS: For my own ends.

2ND CITIZEN: Your own?

CORIOLANUS: Not because I wish to stand up here in this
ridiculous attitude.

3RD CITIZEN: How's that?

CORIOLANUS: I was never one to approach the poor with appeals
for charity.

3RD CITIZEN: You must think that whatever we might choose to
give you, we'd expect something in return.

CORIOLANUS: I'm prepared to go through this for your price; for
a consul's life. And what would you say was that price?

1ST CITIZEN: The price is to ask for it kindly. Understandingly,
helpful; uncondescending.

CORIOLANUS: Kindly? I *have* been kindly, as you call it, and what
else, dispersed more understanding, helpfulness than you've
had public benefits.

2ND CITIZEN: Well, I'll take a chance on you.

CORIOLANUS: A convert, sir. There's a couple.

3RD CITIZEN: This doesn't seem the right way to me to go about it.

2ND CITIZEN: Well, there it is.

(*They go out and are replaced by two more* CITIZENS.

CORIOLANUS *speaks into his loud hailer on the top of the van.*)

CORIOLANUS: This is Coriolanus, your candidate for the consulship.

1ST CITIZEN: You've done all right in some things but very good
in others.

CORIOLANUS: Ah! An enigmatist!

1ST CITIZEN: Oh, you've mopped up the troubles overseas in *your* way. But you don't *do* anything, let alone care anything for us, your own ordinary people.

CORIOLANUS: You should think the more of me for it, for not being indiscriminate. Oh, I will make the right noises to my brothers, my comrades, my people. Will they think the better of me for it? So it seems. They demand reason, reassurances, promises and: policies, those policies you love so dearly; so if you prefer that to my private voice, you shall have it; for I'm not without skill in showing off my policies—like a dancing girl wriggling on the Capitol in front of your tired, old, eager eyes. I can strip off before your very eyes and dissemble very nicely—if a cavorting eunuch's what you're after. *And I* should have known: you are! *I* am your man! Make *me* your consul!

2ND CITIZEN: What's he on about? We only want to *hear* from you. Wages, prices, schemes, rehabilitation work, hours, conditions.

CORIOLANUS: You shall, my friend.

1ST CITIZEN: Hear, hear.

2ND CITIZEN: What are you 'hear, hearing'?

CORIOLANUS: I will deal with these things. And sharply. But you don't want to stand listening to *me*.

BOTH: Good luck, mate.

(*They go out.*)

CORIOLANUS: Good luck, mate . . . Voice of my heart! I'd rather be shot at than go through this knocking on doors for a pair of powerful boots; or scuffling in the streets of Rome. Begging from every Tired Tom and Dozey Dick who wants to put in his few miserable pence. Tradition, the law demands it of us all. Anything can be allowed to happen or rise up if it's only in the name of common tradition. Rather than that, they can stuff their boots up to their elbow and let 'em stay there.

(*Enter three more* CITIZENS. CORIOLANUS *picks up the hailer.*)

Can you hear me? Can you? Hear me? Well, I am peddling myself, and I need *your* voices. Not only mine—to make me consul.

(*Some cheers. Then enter* MENENIUS *and the* TRIBUNES *of the people.*)

CORIOLANUS: You hear that. The People's voice. Isn't that a sound? Enough to gag a man's bowels!

SICINIUS: What's that?

CORIOLANUS: Oh, and women too, madam, or what it is I should call you?

MENENIUS (*hurriedly, seeing trouble*): You've done well. And the tribunes here will endorse you. The rest will be formality, I tell you. Then off to the Senate at long last.

CORIOLANUS: Is this true?

SICINIUS: You have played your part. You will get your consulship by the consent of the people.

CORIOLANUS: Where next? The Senate House?

SICINIUS: The Senate House.

CORIOLANUS: Can I get these things off now?

SICINIUS: You may.

CORIOLANUS: I'll do that right away and feel myself again—if I'm still there.

MENENIUS: I'll come with you. Will *you* come?

BRUTUS: We'll stay down here a while.

SICINIUS: Goodbye, Coriolanus.

(CORIOLANUS *and* MENENIUS *go out*.)

It's all but in his pocket now.

BRUTUS: He didn't give much away . . .

(*Enter the* PLEBIANS.)

SICINIUS: Well, is he our man?

1ST CITIZEN: He's got our vote.

BRUTUS: Let's hope he deserves it.

2ND CITIZEN: Hear, hear, to that. But it seemed to me, he didn't think much of anyone, not himself even. He poked fun at everyone, everything.

3RD CITIZEN: Right. He was having it over us quite openly.

1ST CITIZEN: No. It is his manner, his way of speaking we didn't catch. He doesn't mean it.

2ND CITIZEN: Well, you're the only one to think so. He hardly bothered to explain himself.

SICINIUS: But he must have done.

ALL: No. No. What did we hear!

3RD CITIZEN: All he talked about was something about all being,

I don't remember—being condemned to moments of isolating
oneself, at one time or another in one's life. But what has he
to *SAY*! That's what I'd like to find out. All I know is that
he wants to be consul. Some grudging sweet talk all round
and then that's that! Was this not a mockery!

(CHEERS.)

SICINIUS: Either you were mistaken or, if you were not, then why
did you pledge him your support?

BRUTUS: Couldn't you have said to him that he's the same man
he's always been? That he is, has been, and always will be
against our kind!

(ROARS.)

You should have told him each and every one of the things
he stands for. Not changed! Do you believe: *changed*! You
are conned and conned easily and well he knows it.

SICINIUS: You know his temper. Why didn't you trample on it?
That would have shown you: that would have seen the end
of *his* election.

BRUTUS: Didn't you see one outstretched palm and the other
raising up his finger at you? When he *wanted* you! And do
you think he'll treat you any better for this trick? Wasn't
there one doubtful soul among you?

SICINIUS: Well, what do you say now?

3RD CITIZEN: It's still not fixed. There's time yet to reverse it;
if we've a mind to it.

2ND CITIZEN: Well?

(CHEERS AND ACCLAIM.)

1ST CITIZEN: And I'll double that show of hands in hours.

BRUTUS: Get to it then. Tell your friends they've chosen the wrong
consul; who's against all they've fought for and against. They
have some liberties, let them brandish them.

SICINIUS: Get them altogether. And when they've thought better
of it and realised what they've done, put him to the real
test. Smoke him out. He is there for it. So go to it. Let
him show, and show to *everyone*, what his real opinion is of
you.

BRUTUS: Forgive us for having seemed to stand aside. But the
time came for you to act on your own.

SICINIUS: Yes. Blame it on *us*. But, in the meantime, you've found
   your own true voice.
BRUTUS: Oh, say what you like about *us*. Say we talked you into
   it.
SICINIUS: Change your minds and tell him so and *why*!
   (ROARS. *The* PLEBIANS *go out*.)
BRUTUS: Let them go. It's best to take a risk at this stage.
SICINIUS: We'd better go to the Capitol. In the forefront.

SCENE TWELVE

*Rome. A conference room. Into the room with its long table and rows
of chairs come* CORIOLANUS, MENENIUS, SENATORS, COMINIUS *and*
TITUS LARTIUS.

CORIOLANUS: So Aufidius has made some more new ground.
TITUS: He has. Which was why we had to come to some kind of
   terms quicker.
CORIOLANUS: So then, so then, we are back where we started
   except the Volscians are no doubt better off than ever and
   ready to start up the whole thing again, when it suits them.
COMINIUS: They are worn out, Lord Consul. I hardly think we
   shall see those banners wave again in our lifetime.
CORIOLANUS: Did you see Aufidius?
TITUS: We had a pre-arranged meeting in secret. He was full of
   bile for the Volscians giving up the town so easily as he
   seemed to think. Now he's gone back to Antium.
CORIOLANUS: Did he speak about me?
TITUS: He did indeed.
CORIOLANUS: How? What?
TITUS: The times he had met you; of all the things he'd pawn in
   order to get you.
CORIOLANUS: And he's staying at Antium, you say?
TITUS: Antium. If only I could be given the excuse to go and get
   him back.
   (*Enter* SICINIUS *and* BRUTUS.)

SICINIUS: Stay where you are.

CORIOLANUS: What is this?

BRUTUS: I am warning you. It will be dangerous for you to go out of here.

CORIOLANUS: What has happened?

MENENIUS: The facts?

COMINIUS: Is the vote not as good as his? All but the counting?

BRUTUS: No, Cominius.

CORIOLANUS: So these were children's voices?

1ST SENATOR: Out of the way, tribunes. He's to go to his place.

BRUTUS: They've been roused up against him.

SICINIUS: We wouldn't advise it.

CORIOLANUS: Is this your herd? Has the cat given back their tongues? Their mouths seem empty enough; but own up, aren't you their teeth? Haven't *you* set them on?

MENENIUS: Calm, do be calm.

CORIOLANUS: This is all a trumped up thing; and it will get bigger. First it was to flout the law and when that wasn't frightening enough for you, you take on yourselves to maim and injure anyone in sight. And why? Because policy— yes, policy—dominates and is . . . wonderfully afraid. That's your game, isn't it?

BRUTUS: Not a worse one than the way you go about yours.

CORIOLANUS: Why should I elect to be a consul? Let life do me so much ill that I'll end up like you and be a tribune.

SICINIUS: These are your true colours.

MENENIUS: Let's try to be calm.

COMINIUS: People feel they have been abused, stirred up, led to believe things that were not so. This lack of openness doesn't become Rome. Nor does Coriolanus deserve to be brushed aside.

CORIOLANUS: Talk to me of wages, prices! I spoke to them once and I will again.

MENENIUS: Not now, not now.

1ST SENATOR: Not in your present mood.

CORIOLANUS: *Now; I will*! 'My good friends', I crave their pardon; each and every one of them, changeable, aggressive, craven, every one of them. Don't let them think of me as a flatterer and therefore fit to govern them. Let's not throw away everything we have sown and tended for a few rebellious weeds, and weeds I do mean, by letting them in too far.

MENENIUS: Well, no more.

1ST SENATOR: No, no more words for heaven's sake.

CORIOLANUS: What! No more! Why shouldn't my lungs be allowed to go on coining words until they burst, as sure as hell they will?

BRUTUS: You talk of people as if you were God, expressly brought up to punish as if you'd no diseases of your own at all.

SICINIUS: The sooner it's made clear to them, the better.

MENENIUS: What, what! His anger?

CORIOLANUS: Anger? If I were as patient as my deepest sleep, dear God, it would still be from my *mind*.

SICINIUS: Then it's a mind that shall stay where it is——

CORIOLANUS: Is! 'Shall stay where it is'? Did you hear this frightening black-faced lady! Did you hear!

COMINIUS: She was out of order.

CORIOLANUS: 'Shall'! Oh, you nice, foolish men. You plodding reckless Senators. This lady here has so many heads she cannot live with them all, which is why she chooses to lose them in a mob of others. If you think power lies there, then give in to it now. If not, do something about it and at once. Would you let them pitch their 'shall' against yours? This popular 'shall' against the gentlest amd most civilized society the world has seen! It makes my bones ache to see such a situation; when two sides are both too weak to assume supremacy; and how revolution will come between the two of them and destroy the lot.

COMINIUS: We must be off.

MENENIUS: Yes, no more of that.

CORIOLANUS: I'll give my reasons when asked for 'em. What can you give to the Siciniuses of Rome to satisfy their prudish imaginations? 'We are the strongest because we are the most, to hell with the best, we do not acknowledge such a possibility. What we make, we shall *employ*.' Not invent, mark you, what we *make*, look into the future to. They talk of this sweat and that's their most important product—and they smell it over half the world. Well, let them take it over; let it *be* theirs!

MENENIUS: That's enough.

BRUTUS: Enough for us!

CORIOLANUS: No, not enough for me. Well, let's get to your policies; the ones without purpose—except to indulge the worst of you and pacify the rest.

SICINIUS: Your mouth is your undoing, my friend. Have you not heard of such a thing as reticence in politicking?

CORIOLANUS: I have not learned from you. You are too trivial for reticence; otherwise you would disappear up your own supporters. In a rebellion like this, we must live under the law or there will be no life for the most of us.

SICINIUS: Or change it.

CORIOLANUS: Change it! Administer it. You could not own a stall in the market without state assistance.

SICINIUS: This a consul? No!

(*Enter an* AEDILE (*a sort of* PEOPLE'S POLICEMAN.))

(*to* PEOPLE'S POLICEMAN): Take him. Get the city all together.

(*Exit* PEOPLE'S POLICEMAN.)

CORIOLANUS: Go on, get them together, 'policeman'—policeman of the piss poor! Get off out of it, hairy charm-pits.

PATRICIANS: We'll stand surety for him.

(*The* TRIBUNES *attack* COMINIUS. CORIOLANUS *intervenes, grabbing them.*)

CORIOLANUS: Get off before I play marbles with the two of you!

SICINIUS: Help!

(*Confusion as police and troops arrive. Roars and singing from outside.*)

SCENE THIRTEEN

A public square. Crowds and noise. As before, only more so. Everyone from Rome.

ALL: Tribunes!—Patricians!—Citizens!—Ay, ay! Sicinius! Brutus! Coriolanus! Workers! People!

MENENIUS: Will you listen. I can't make myself heard if you won't listen. I can't speak. You, tribunes, speak to them. Hold back, Coriolanus. Sicinius, you are the one they want to hear!

SICINIUS: Comrades! People! Listen!

CROWD: Go on then! Get on with it! Let's hear some bit of sense. (*etc.*)

SICINIUS: Just this: you're about to lose your freedom, that's all. Marcius will have the lot off you. Yes, Caius Marcius, whom you even chose to elect as consul!

MENENIUS: Now then, now. This is the way to rioting, not public discussion of the issue.

1ST SENATOR: This way we'll just end up a flattened city and nothing else.

SICINIUS: What's the city but the people in it?

ALL: The people are the city. We are the people—CITY! We are the people—CITY! We are the people—CITY!
(*They are held back. Just.*)

BRUTUS: And who represents them, that city?

ALL: You do! CITY! CITY! CITY!

MENENIUS: And so you will go on doing.

COMINIUS: This is the way to bring us all down to a new age of desolation and darkness.

SICINIUS: You hear that? Darkness he calls it. What is to us?

ALL: Light. L-I-G-H-T! Light!

BRUTUS: MARCIUS out!

SICINIUS: You hear that!

ALL: MAR-CI-US OUT!

SICINIUS: Get him.

ALL (CITIZENS): Get, down, MARCIUS. Out, Marcius, O-U-T, *out*!

MENENIUS: Give me a word, I ask you!

BRUTUS: We know your 'old school'. Grab him.

MENENIUS: Someone help MARCIUS.

CROWD: Get him! Get him! (*etc.*)
(*Confusion as people and POLICEMEN, TROOPS confront each other. Howling, people trod underfoot. The crowd surges forward but is scattered.*)

CORIOLANUS: We are not without friends.

COMINIUS: Let's get out of it.

(*They go under escort.*)

MENENIUS: Go home. All of you. In the name of Rome and your children and their children. We shall sit down and talk this out or give up everything.

SICINIUS (*to* MOB): What? Coriolanus? Well?

MENENIUS: Your consul.

SICINIUS: What consul?

BRUTUS: He, consul?

CROWD: No, no, no, NO. Out, out, out out!

(MENENIUS *goes out.*)

SICINIUS: Oh, we'll talk.

(*Cheers from* MOB.)

SCENE FOURTEEN

Rome. The house of CORIOLANUS. *Enter* CORIOLANUS *with* MENENIUS, SENATORS.

CORIOLANUS: My mother's disapproval *does* surprise me. Even though it's so obvious by now. She was always the first to support me—even in her best misunderstanding.

(*Enter* VOLUMNIA.)

Well, now, Mother, I'm talking of you. Why do you want me to be milder then? You, you to want me false to my nature? Rather than take a stab at what I am?

VOLUMNIA: Oh, Caius, I want only what is best for you and what's best for you must be best for Rome.

CORIOLANUS: Oh, enough of that!

VOLUMNIA: You can be the man you are without striving this much. You would have done better to show less, not more.

CORIOLANUS: Let 'em hang.

VOLUMNIA: Oh, and burn too.

MENENIUS: Come, come, you're indiscreet to the point of lunacy. But there's still time to make amends. There always is.

SENATOR: If you don't we shall all be brought down, if the city itself doesn't disappear for good.

VOLUMNIA: Listen to them, Caius. My heart's just the same as yours, but it's detachment's still there——

MENENIUS: Well said. He must address himself to the situation as it is, not as he would *have* it.

CORIOLANUS: What do you want me to do?

MENENIUS: Take it all back and do it with conviction. They are not fooled easily.

CORIOLANUS: For *them*. I could not do it for my wife, my son, my life. Would you get me to do it for *them*?

VOLUMNIA: You are too passionate and too pedantic with it. Like they say wrongly women—only it's not so.

CORIOLANUS: Too passionate or too pedantic?

VOLUMNIA: Neither. I won't argue with you in this mood. But I've heard you say yourself honour and policy can go together without necessarily debasing one another.

CORIOLANUS: I must have been drunk, ironic; both; that or you weren't listening to my real voice.

MENENIUS: Listen to her.

VOLUMNIA: After all, if you can see your way to bluffing so successfully in war, why not now, when far more's at stake?

CORIOLANUS: Why pursue it?

VOLUMNIA: Because now is not the time to indulge in passion but talk in terms that everyone will accept and understand. There's no dishonour in bringing the city to just terms merely by using the right form of words. How can you play emotion with so much *future*? I would do *far* more. For your wife, your son, these upright senators, all of them. Do you want just to impress louts with your intransigence? They don't know what it means!

MENENIUS: She's right. But we must make a move while there's still time.

VOLUMNIA: My son. Do it. We, who know you the most, we'll know what you are doing *and* why.

MENENIUS: Do as she says, and we still have a chance . . .

VOLUMNIA: Go and look as if you have been overruled. It's not beyond you.

(*Enter* COMINIUS.)

COMINIUS: It's all uproar. Only Coriolanus can damp it down.
Even so, it looks like being too late.

MENENIUS: A few words . . . The right *appearance*.

VOLUMNIA: He must, he will. I beg you, say you will . . .

CORIOLANUS: Go out there to lie? A lie that's *mine* for always?
Well, I'll do it. I'll put on the right face, the familiar
expressions, the flattened, conciliatory vowels. I will, what
is it, agree, no, not agree, *plead* for arbitration.

COMINIUS: We'll all help you.

VOLUMNIA: You have done things before you hated. Do this, just
for this last time.

CORIOLANUS: Well then, I must do it. Don't press your point,
mother, I'll dissemble better than the best of you.

VOLUMNIA: Do as you like.
(*Exit* VOLUMNIA.)

COMINIUS: The tribunes are waiting. Be prepared indeed to
conciliate, be mild. They are watching for every flicker.
Heaven knows what new things they've up their sleeves.

CORIOLANUS: Right. 'Mildly' is the word. Let's get it over with.
I have a few unplayed tricks of my own.

MENENIUS: But mildly, remember.

CORIOLANUS: Well, mildly be it then. Mildly.

SCENE FIFTEEN

Rome. The Forum. SICINIUS *and* BRUTUS *raised above the mob. Crescendo
as they appear above everyone.*

CROWD: We want Marcius!
We want Marcius!
We want Marcius!

BRUTUS: He's coming.

SICINIUS: Who with?

BRUTUS: Menenius and his old mob.

SICINIUS: Have you a count of votes?

BRUTUS: It's all done.

SICINIUS: Each area?

BRUTUS: Every one. That matters.

SICINIUS: Get them all in close. And when I say: 'It's the voice
of the people'—whether it be for a fine, banishment, or death;
if I say 'Fine' yell 'Fine', if 'Let him have it', then 'Let him
have it', 'Kill him' and so on. Understood? Death in revolution can't be called 'murder' afterwards. So, look to it.

BRUTUS: Will do. The stewards know already. If he's not on the
boil already, they'll soon turn him up. He's not used to being
answered in his own insulting coin. Once we've got him good
and riled, there's no going back. He'll put his heart, where
his neck is, on the chopper.

(*Enter* CORIOLANUS, MENENIUS, COMINIUS *and others.*)

SICINIUS: So, there he is at long last.

MENENIUS: Calm, now.

CORIOLANUS: I have promised. I will try: for Rome.

1ST SENATOR: Amen, amen.

MENENIUS: Good lad!

SICINIUS: Listen to me, hear out your tribunes. Calm it down.
Now. Please. I ask you!

CORIOLANUS: First, let me speak.

SICINIUS: Well now.

BRUTUS: His lordship's come to talk to you!

CORIOLANUS: Do we, can we, come to some terms in, in this
place?

SICINIUS: I merely ask that you put your case to these citizens
who've gathered here, with their lawful officers. And that you
accept their reply. That's all.

CORIOLANUS: Very well.

MENENIUS: You see? He's served us all in our different ways.

CORIOLANUS: Only with laughter?

MENENIUS: Just so. He doesn't mince words. And not a bad thing
in these times, *I* say!

COMINIUS: Get on with it.

CORIOLANUS: Why have you changed your minds and turned
against me so late in the game?

SICINIUS: You tell *us!*

CORIOLANUS: I'll try.

SICINIUS: They've discovered at last that all moderation would end
  with you.
CORIOLANUS: And *you*!
SICINIUS: I love this city. Most of all, I love its people. You are
  its traitor; their traitor and they have found you out.
CORIOLANUS: How? Traitor!
MENENIUS: Mild, mild, you said.
CORIOLANUS: Call me traitor, you dead droppings of old cant.
  You lie. You lie in your green teeth!
SICINIUS: You hear him? Such moderation . . .
MOB: *Do* him. Do him! Kill him! Kill him! Kill, (*etc.*)
SICINIUS: Enough, cowards. Enough, for we've seen enough.
  Haven't WE SEEN *enough* of this—MAN!
BRUTUS: It's true he's done some things for Rome.
CORIOLANUS: What do you know about it?
BRUTUS: I know what I'm talking about.
CORIOLANUS: You!
MENENIUS: So much for your promise to your mother.
COMINIUS: Now, listen a moment——
CORIOLANUS: I wouldn't take *their* say-so for NUPPENCE one way or
  the other. I wouldn't give 'em the sweat from my balls.
SICINIUS: Let him go before he's killed—and it wouldn't be
  unjust——
MOB: Send him off! Take him off! Get lost! And for damned good
  and forever, (*etc*).
COMINIUS: Listen!
SICINIUS: You heard the verdict clear enough. Again?
  (ROAR.)
SICINIUS: Right. He's done for. No more talk. We have heard it
  all before from your like.
BRUTUS: Right. That's it then.
MOB: That's it! That's it! (*etc.*)
CORIOLANUS: You common cry of curs. You take up my air.
  Banish me? *I* banish *you*! Stay here in your slum. And strike.
  Communicate. Get shaken with rumours; fads; modishness;
  greed; fashion; your clannishness; your lives in depth. May
  you, but you won't, one minute of that depth, know desola-
  tion. May your enemies barter and exchange you coolly in

57

their own better market-places . . . I have seen the *future* . . .
here . . . and it doesn't work! *I* turn my back. There is a
world *elsewhere*!

(*He goes off, borne away by his supporters and sorely harassed
escort.* CORIOLANUS *sings down at them a parody of* 'The Red
Flag'.)

> 'The Working Class
> Can Kiss My Arse
> And keep their Red
> Rag flying high.'

(*He is swept off, pursued by the furious mob.*)

Act Two

SCENE ONE

Airport. CORIOLANUS, VOLUMNIA, VIRGILIA, MENENIUS, COMINIUS.
CORIOLANUS *is embracing* VIRGILIA.

CORIOLANUS: Come, that's enough. Farewells really are a lifetime. Whereas 'hullo, darling's 's gone in minutes and silent
disappointment after. Come along, Mother, you've always
been only too good on these occasions—away to school,
the army, death beds, funerals, you've been an admirable
Goodbyer. I thought you'd taught me pretty well.

VIRGILIA: Oh, Caius, Caius.

CORIOLANUS: I beg you——

VOLUMNIA: You giggled when I used to talk of red pestilence;
the trades of Rome; all occupations gone but war and
bargaining and faction——

CORIOLANUS: What's this? You should miss me when I'm *here*,
not gone or about to go. Be the same as ever was, Mother.
Cominius, my friend, this will all change and sort itself out
as it has before . . . Goodbye, Virgilia . . . Menenius, soppy
old thing, I always knew it. My old chief, my friend . . .
Look after them all. I know you will. Mother, you know that
my worst setbacks have stirred you on. Not cast you down.
Don't think I go my own way easily or lightly. More talked
about and forgotten . . . and not seen. I will do more than
the usual, as you know, unless I'm sold out, who knows how?

VOLUMNIA: My very first son, where will you go? Take Cominius
with you. Make some plan first rather than expose yourself
to every wildcat waiting in every corner for you.

CORIOLANUS: Oh, God!

COMINIUS: I'll come with you. Somewhere we can hole up and

draw up a proper campaign. So, when the time comes,
as it will, when they need you back, there'll be no other man
left in the world they'll turn to. They'll soon see what's
lacking in them.

CORIOLANUS: No, Cominius, it's too late for you to follow me on
this kind of jaunt. Just see me off. Come, Virgilia, Mother,
Menenius. Just see the going of me and go home for a
gossip and a drink or two. You shall hear from me. And
never any differently than before.

MENENIUS: Exactly. I still wish *I* were young enough to come
with you.

CORIOLANUS: Give me your hand. Come.

(*They go out.*)

SCENE TWO

Rome. Airport. SICINIUS *and* BRUTUS.

SICINIUS: They can all go home. He's gone and that's that. The
top brass are pretty fed up with us, but, of course, they've
sided with him all along; *and* at his extremest, though they'd
dare not say as much.

BRUTUS: Now we've shown the support we've got, we can afford
to seem more amenable.

SICINIUS: We can *all* go home and say the great fanatic who
represents no responsible opinion has gone and we are back
to where we were and can start again.

BRUTUS: That's his mother.

(*Enter* VOLUMNIA, VIRGILIA *and* MENENIUS.)

SICINIUS: Let's avoid her.

BRUTUS: Why?

SICINIUS: They say she's gone quite cracked.

BRUTUS: They've seen us. Keep going.

VOLUMNIA: Ah, there you are. Your come-uppance hasn't been
called yet, but it will.

MENENIUS: Don't raise your voice. It's pointless.

VOLUMNIA: Do you think I am not trying——

(*in tears.*)
Or they'd *hear*——
No, you *will* hear.
(*to* BRUTUS.)
Going?

VIRGILIA (*to* SICINIUS): Yes, and you stay too. I wish I could
   have said so to my husband.

SICINIUS: What are you then? Mankind? Or something?

VOLUMNIA: That was a shoddy answer. My father was mankind,
   if you like. You think you have the wit to keep my
   Coriolanus out of Rome, who has done more, thought more,
   been more——

SICINIUS: Not that! God preserve us that!

VOLUMNIA: More than your old, reach-me-down words. I tell you.
   I tell you what—no, go. No, you shall stay. You are not fit
   to meet him face to face whatever world you found yourselves
   in.

SICINIUS: So?

VIRGILIA: So? He'll see *you* out!

VOLUMNIA: Bastards and all. Oh, what has happened to him!

MENENIUS: Come, come . . .

SICINIUS: It's a pity he did not go on as he seemed to start—on
   all our behalves.

BRUTUS: It is.

VOLUMNIA: It is! It was you who roused them up. Like tom cats
   in the night who know as little of what he is as I know of
   what lies ahead of us.

BRUTUS: Let's go.

VOLUMNIA: Yes, you go! You must be feeling very brave today.
   But before you do, listen to this: as far as all Rome is finer
   than you each in your little houses, this lady's husband is
   better than any one of you.

BRUTUS: Well, we'll go.

SICINIUS: Why stay to be harangued by a dotty old woman!
   (TRIBUNES *exit.*)

VOLUMNIA: And my fingers with you! If I had nothing else to do
   but think of alternatives to *them*! If only I could set eyes on
   them once a day, it might help.

MENENIUS: They got your message, madam. Shall we dine together?
VOLUMNIA: I can't eat except what's in here for them. Very well,
let's get going. We can't stand wasting time.
MENENIUS: Oh, dear.

(*They all go.*)

SCENE THREE

Antium. Near AUFIDIUS's *headquarters.* CORIOLANUS *comes out of a
drab-looking pub, dressed like a working man. A man follows him out.*

CORIOLANUS: Good evening to you.
MAN: And to you.
CORIOLANUS: Tell me, if it's possible, where's Aufidius?
MAN: Aufidius?
CORIOLANUS: He *is* in Antium?
MAN: Everyone knows that. He'll be having a right old carouse
with the best of 'em tonight.
CORIOLANUS: Tell me, where can I make contact with him?
MAN: Who wants to know?
CORIOLANUS: Someone; someone uniquely placed to get him what
he's always set his heart on.

(MAN *hesitates then he scribbles on a piece of paper, which he
hands to* CORIOLANUS.)

Thank you.
MAN: Forget you saw me.

(*He disappears into the shadows.* CORIOLANUS *reads the piece
of paper.*)

CORIOLANUS: Here I am, hating my own birthplace and ending
up in Antium with a slip of paper. Oh, world, what slippery
terms! Oh, I can find this place. If he shoots me down,
he'll have done well for himself. If not, *I* can do things for
him even now.

SCENE FOUR

Antium. A room in AUFIDIUS's *headquarters.* CORIOLANUS *is being restrained by three of* AUFIDIUS's *men.*

AUFIDIUS: Who the devil's this?

1ST MAN: I'll beat the bejesus out of him.

AUFIDIUS: Who let him get in at all?

1ST MAN: Nobody, Aufidius.

AUFIDIUS: Oh, nobody is it? Then nobody let go of him and nobody let him out! Where do you come from? What do you want? Speak up. What's your name?

CORIOLANUS (*unmuffling*): If, Tullus, you still can't guess who I am, take me for what I am: necessity!

AUFIDIUS: Name?

CORIOLANUS: Not one that's liked much by the Volscians; least of all by you.

AUFIDIUS: Your name. Your clothes don't fool me, but I can't see the face.

CORIOLANUS: Then prepare yourself. Still not know?

AUFIDIUS: I've told you. Your name, damn you.

CORIOLANUS: Caius Marcius. Or, Coriolanus, to you. For that's my name since I think we last had the pleasure. That surname's all I have to show for the services I gave to my grateful country. So much . . . A name for the hatred you've lived off for the likes of me. A name . . . Coriolanus. All that's left to me before being whooped out of Rome. Which: is how I end up here with you. Oh, believe me, not to save my life, for this is the last place I would come to if I were merely hanging on to something I never had much care for and still less now. I am here for, for miserable spite; no more no less. If you want your revenge for Corioli, you *could* take it now. Then you'd best do it now rather than gossip with me. Otherwise, think how you can use me against your enemy— against troops. Battalions of 'em. Even *you* might do with *my* spleen. Think on it. Still, if the idea is beyond your Volscian folk visions, it's beyond me too; even the hatred I

once felt for you and all your vicious kind. There *is* nothing
left but leading *your* kind.

AUFIDIUS: Oh, Marcius, Marcius! What are you doing to me!
From your lips. Here!

(*They embrace.*)

I loved my wife when I first clapped eyes on her, but my
heart's not run such a dance since she crossed my own
doorway. Marcius, Caius Marcius!

(*They embrace again.*)

Why, I tell you we shall put such a force in the field the
world will be *astonished*. I have dreamt of killing you with
my own hands so many times, I no longer even wake up with
the sweat unless my wife begs me to stop thrashing about.
Marcius, if we had no other quarrel with Rome than that
she'd slung you out, that, that would be enough for me.
Come in, come in, meet everyone. We are making plans
at the moment for the outskirts; if not actually Rome
itself.

CORIOLANUS: God bless you.

AUFIDIUS: You are perfect. Perfect. Who knows better, *feels* best!
You will draw up the tactics, morale strategies. You know,
you know the gaps, the weaknesses . . . Let me show you off
to your new comrades. Welcome! A better friend even than a
good enemy. Oh, Marcius, this is a great, great thing that has
happened. Give me your hand!

(*They go out, arms round one another.*)

1ST MAN: I don't see this at all.

2ND MAN: Nor I. Still, he's a rare man.

1ST MAN: He is. But Aufidius is worth six of him.

2ND MAN: Who can tell?

1ST MAN: We'll see.

(*Enter* THIRD MAN.)

3RD MAN: I don't like it. He's got them all in there listening to
him—and Aufidius in the middle, like the rest. He's more
hopping mad than *we* ever were.

2ND MAN: Then we shall have the 'old times' stirring again. Let's
get on with it, I say. Fighting's better than this sitting around.
A fine campaign *this*. Action is move and muscle, peace is

just lethargy and drowsy blood. Nothing to do but make
unwanted babies in some strange place.

3RD MAN: Perhaps we'll see the Romans done like they did the
Volscians. Here's to it. We're coming. Good comrades!
(*They dash out.*)

SCENE FIVE

Rome. Conference room. SICINIUS *and* BRUTUS.

SICINIUS: There's no news of him and I don't expect any. Mark
'rendered harmless'. Everything's settled back into the old
ways so quickly. His old friends are quite put out by it all.
They'd rather have had the place in turmoil even if it cost
them money *and* what they own; and we all know how much
that means to 'em. Apparently, happy workers make them
feel more uneasy than unfriendly ones.

BRUTUS: We had our show-down at the right time.
(*Enter* MENENIUS.)

BRUTUS: Well, and here's Menenius to prove it.

SICINIUS: Indeed. Oh, he's got *very* friendly lately . . . Hallo to
you, sir.

MENENIUS: Hallo.

SICINIUS: Your Coriolanus doesn't seem missed much except by
a few friends. We seem to survive without him. I wonder
what he would think if he were here.

MENENIUS: It certainly seems to have settled down. But how much
better it could have been if he could have only yielded here
and there.

SICINIUS: Have you heard where he is?

MENENIUS: No, I hear nothing. His wife and mother have heard
nothing either.

BRUTUS: Caius Marcius was good at what he was most good at.
War and just, oh, general hostility. But, added to that, he
was, let's see: insolent, overcome with pride, ambitious
beyond all thinking, self-loving——

SICINIUS: Aiming for himself and one self alone. Even without support.

MENENIUS: I think that's an unfair assessment.

SICINIUS: You'd have soon found it so if he had ever become consul.

BRUTUS: I think we can say we did well to prevent that and Rome can sleep safely without him.

(*Enter* MESSENGER *with papers which he hands to* MENENIUS.)

MENENIUS (*reading*): It's Aufidius. Just what I feared. With Marcius gone, he's come out of his hole as I knew he would.

SICINIUS: Marcius? Aufidius? This is all rumour. The Volscians wouldn't dare take us on again.

MENENIUS: Can't be! We know very well that it *can*. Three times it's happened in my own lifetime.

BRUTUS: It's not possible.

MESSENGER: More news is coming in all the time. No-one knows quite what's happening or what to do. It's being said openly, how probable I don't know, that Marcius has joined up with Aufidius; they've joined up together against Rome and planned such horrors beyond—well, contemplation.

SICINIUS: This makes sense.

BRUTUS: Thinking that the weakest ones among us will welcome Marcius back again on any terms . . .

SICINIUS: Exactly.

MENENIUS: I don't believe it. He and Aufidius are too much for each other.

(*Enter* COMINIUS.)

COMINIUS: You must go to the Senate at once. An incredible force led by, yes, Caius Marcius and Aufidius with him has landed already and is hurtling at this moment towards the city and with hardly any resistance from us. Oh, you have done well, I hope you are pleased with yourselves. The place will fall on your heads and the rest of us with you. Oh, you have done well, believe me.

MENENIUS: And this is true about Marcius and the Volscians?

COMINIUS: He's like a *god* to them. He leads them against us like something out of hell, only better. They chase us like schoolboys after butterflies; which is all we are, according to their book.

MENENIUS: Well, you *have* all done well, you and your fighting workers, you revolutionaries, you brawny slogan turners. What about you now then?

COMINIUS: He'll shake Rome about your ears.

BRUTUS: Is this really true?

COMINIUS: I promise you, you won't find out otherwise, anywhere. Everything is going down in front of him. And who can blame him? Your *enemies* have found something in him.

MENENIUS: We're finished unless he chooses otherwise.

COMINIUS: And who shall ask for it? The Tribunes can't. They've no real power. They've been shown up for what they are. Even if his best friend should say, please be good to Rome, you think they would get a show of less hatred now?

MENENIUS: You are right. If he were setting fire to my own house, I wouldn't have the face to say, please don't. You've done well, you've done well, as you meant to do from the beginning.

COMINIUS (*to* TRIBUNES): What you've brought on Rome! Even our worst times were never so terrible as this. And helpless.

BOTH TRIBUNES: No, not us . . . (*etc.*)

MENENIUS: Then who was it? Are you saying it was *us*? We loved him for what he was and could have been, but like the miserable beasts we are, we gave in to your mob and let them hoot him out of the city.

COMINIUS: But I think you'll find they'll roar him in again. Tullus Aufidius, ah—only just less a personality than Coriolanus, takes his cue as if he were some mere assistant. And against all this, we have—what?

(MENENIUS *looks out of the window*.)

MENENIUS: Here they come. Here come the mobs now. Aufidius? With Coriolanus? You are the ones who howled and voted for the exiling of him. Now he's coming back with his own army and as many of you will yell out 'welcome back' as hurled him out. Never mind. If he could burn us, every one of us, like a huge coal in the universe, we'd deserve it. You're good things, you and your voices. You've done well with them with your linked arms and trying to storm the Capitol. And *we* let you do it!

COMINIUS: Oh yes, what else?

(COMINIUS *and* MENENIUS *go out accompanied by the*
MESSENGER.)

BRUTUS: I don't like this.

SICINIUS: Nor I.

BRUTUS: Let's go to the Capitol. I'd give everything I have if this
were just rumour.

SICINIUS: I don't think it is. Let's go.

(*They go out.*)

SCENE SIX

Enter AUFIDIUS *with one of his lieutenants.*

AUFIDIUS: They still flock to that Roman.

LIEUTENANT: I don't know what it is about him but our men use
his name like saying grace before a meal. This is not good
for you . . . that your own men——

AUFIDIUS: I can't help it now. It's too early to take steps. Certainly
he's taken wing. Even to me, more than I thought he would
when we first clutched each other but he's the self same man.
One must excuse what can't be changed—while it suits.

LIEUTENANT: I still wish, sir—I mean for your own sake—that
you'd not gone into double harness. Perhaps it would have
been better to have done the whole thing yourself or even to
have let him get on with it on his own.

AUFIDIUS: I know what you mean well enough. But you can be
sure of that, that when his account comes in, he has no idea
of what *I* can charge against him. Oh, I will agree with you
that to the Volscian state he does seem a brilliant manager,
does all he can and leaves no possibility unexamined; and up
till now, he has done what was promised. Still, something
will be left undone and that will either break his neck or
mine, when we come to the adding up.

LIEUTENANT: Do you think, sir, that he'll take Rome on his own?
Everywhere's surrendering to him before he starts. The

nobility of Rome are in his pocket; so too are the Senators and Patricians. As for the Tribunes, no soldiers they and as for the people, they'll be as keen to mark their yeses in the right place as they were to mark 'no' before.

AUFIDIUS: Oh, I think he'll be to Rome what a pirhana is to an overfleshed human. It's the nature of them both, as he was their honoured servant but then couldn't keep his balance. Whether it was pride brought on by unbroken boyish fame, who knows, but he was lucky in it, whatever it was it may have been. Perhaps he had defective judgment in following up; certainly he had the chances. But whatever, this was a right royal rising up of one man we've not seen the like of— not in our time; at any rate. But even in all this he was feared and hated more than *anybody*. Can you think of anyone else it was like? Everything he had going for him— it was quite enough to gag on and eventually choke. So whatever value any one of us may have is: no more than what the time puts on to it, and power, however comfortable for its run to sit in, is a pretty hard coffin to lie in. One fire drives out one fire; one nail one nail; rights foundered by rights; strength by strength; they all fail. Let's go. When, Caius, Rome is yours, you will never have been so poor, for I think then you might belong to *me*.

SCENE SEVEN

Rome. Conference room. MENENIUS, COMINIUS, SICINIUS *and* BRUTUS.

MENENIUS: No, I'll not go to see him. You have heard what he said about me; I was once his commander. I loved him in a most, a most particular way. He called me his father once, but—so what now? You go, you that got rid of him. Kneel down before his headquarters and crawl your way back into his mercy if you can. No, if he was reluctant to listen to Cominius, I'll stay at home.

COMINIUS: He didn't want to know me.

MENENIUS: You hear that?

COMINIUS: He did call me by my first name once. I turned on the
times we've had together, the good ones and the bloody ones.
Coriolanus: he wouldn't answer to that name. In fact, no
names. He was a kind of nothing, nameless; without title;
until he had burned a new one for himself out of Rome.

MENENIUS: Oh yes, you Tribunes, you've done your work well.
We shall make a good memorial.

COMINIUS: I tried reminding him how gracious it is for someone
like him to forgive but he said he would treat it just like
any other petition among the rest.

MENENIUS: What else did he say?

SICINIUS: I know this, that if you would go to him, you could do
more than any army we might have or any politician.

MENENIUS: No.

SICINIUS: Please.

MENENIUS: To do what?

SICINIUS: Only you can save Rome from Marcius.

MENENIUS: Well, and what if Marcius sends me packing like
Cominius here, not even listened to—what then? Just another
late friend shot down with one of his glances. What if that
happens?

SICINIUS: Then you will have done all you can . . .

MENENIUS: Very well. I'll try. I think he *may* listen to me. From
Cominius's account, it may well be that he was not approached
at the right time, or mood or something, not fed or overtired.
I'll try and see to it that the circumstances are a bit better
this time. If I think the time *is* right, I'll talk to him like
the old days.

BRUTUS: You know what a sort of maze his heart is but you do
at least know the way.

MENENIUS: I'll do my best with him. How it turns out is another
thing. I'll report as soon as I can.

(*Exit* MENENIUS.)

COMINIUS: He won't listen to him.

SICINIUS: Won't?

COMINIUS: I tell you he sits up to his ears in admiration; with
blood in both eyes and nothing but Rome will catch either

of them. There's no appealing to him. He just told me to go
and sent me off without a word. No word after and nothing
about what he would or wouldn't do. No discussions even,
there *is* nothing left. Oh, there's his wife and mother. I
believe they have plans for trying to reason with him but
I don't set much store by that. However, we shall see.
(*They go out.*)

SCENE EIGHT

CORIOLANUS'*s headquarters in front of Rome.* MENENIUS *is under guard.*

MENENIUS: You, you, listen to me.
   (*Enter* CORIOLANUS *and* AUFIDIUS.)
CORIOLANUS: What's the matter?
MENENIUS: You see, you can't keep me from my own Coriolanus.
   (*to* CORIOLANUS) Oh, my boy, my dear boy. What are you
   preparing for us? Look, I'm here to talk to you. I wasn't
   coming but then I was told there was only myself left. I've
   been blown out of Rome by petitions!
CORIOLANUS: Go away.
MENENIUS: What! Away!
CORIOLANUS: I no longer know you. Wife, mother, child, I wish
   to know nothing *of* you. My interests are in other places.
   Friends, family, lovers, we may have been, but that is past,
   so get along with you. My deafness is more powerful than
   your voice, I promise you. You'll have a safe conduct, I shall
   see to that. Otherwise, I want to hear nothing from you,
   you understand, *nothing*. This man Aufidius is my comrade.
   Look at him, and remember it. You see, Aufidius?
AUFIDIUS: Oh, you are loyal.
   (*The* GUARDS *hustle out* MENENIUS *with their automatics.*
   CORIOLANUS *and* AUFIDIUS *sit down.*)
CORIOLANUS: Tomorrow Rome itself, his own home, will be
   bombarded. My good friend, I hope you'll tell your Volscians
   how I've dealt with these people.

AUFIDIUS: You have been impeccable.

CORIOLANUS: This last old man; it was not easy sending him back to Rome; he always held me up like a son to him. He was their last resource. Well, after him, no more, from state or friends or anybody.

(*There is a noise from outside.*)

I suppose that's one more delegation trying to racket its way in. Well, that's the last.

(*Enter* VIRGILIA, VOLUMNIA *and* YOUNG MARCIUS.)

(*to* AUFIDIUS) It's Virgilia. And my mother and the boy. Well, enough of that. Oh, my mother bows, does she? Now that she wants something that can't be given. Even my young boy's put on a face which he thinks can't be denied. Let the Volscians plough up Rome and harrow all Italy: I'll never be such a moulting *animal* as to give in to instinct; but stand up here as if a man were creator of himself; and knew no other family or friend . . .

VIRGILIA: My dearest.

CORIOLANUS: These are not the same eyes you saw last time in Rome.

VIRGILIA: Seeing us here in this way makes you say this.

CORIOLANUS: Like a played out actor I've forgotten my lines. Forgive me, but don't ask me in return to forgive our Romans. God, I babble on just at the sight of two women.

VOLUMNIA: It's we who ask your forgiveness.

CORIOLANUS: What's this? You ask me?

VOLUMNIA: Your son, your wife, myself, we all do.

CORIOLANUS: Stop. Don't put this display on for me. You vulgarize yourselves. Don't ask me to give up my army or make terms with Rome, Rome's workers. Don't tell me I'm unnatural. Above all, don't reason with me.

VOLUMNIA: Oh, no more, no *more*. You've said you won't give us anything. All we've already asked is denied. But we still ask all the same. Even if it does do no more than harden your outline for the world to make sure. So listen to us.

CORIOLANUS: Aufidius and all you other Volscians, listen. Mark for yourselves: for I hear nothing from Rome that's in private.

(*to* VOLUMNIA) Well?

VOLUMNIA: Would you seriously have us look on silently and watch
the husband, son, the father, tear his country's bowels out!
For myself, son, I don't intend to wait to see the outcome of
this war. If I can't persuade you to your own natural good
grace, then trample on me first.

VIRGILIA: Yes, and me too, and this boy. So much for keeping
your name.

YOUNG MARCIUS: He won't trample on me. I'll run away and then
when I'm bigger, I'll go back and fight him.

(CORIOLANUS *clutches* MARCIUS's *shoulders.*)

CORIOLANUS: It is not necessary for me to see any of you. I have
sat here too long.

VOLUMNIA: No, don't go in this way. You know, my son, the
general, the end of any war's uncertain, but this much is
certain, that if you do overcome Rome, there will be no name
like Coriolanus written in it for *you*. All that will be said is
fine he may have been but his last expedition was no less of
a ruin than his own country. Think of a name for that! Have
you nothing to say? Do you think it a good thing for a man
like yourself only to remember wrong? Virgilia, speak to him.
Your crying means *nothing* to him. Speak up, boy: perhaps
your tears can move him a bit more than we can. He lets
me stand in front of him like a beggar. You have never shown
your mother any courtesy, or perhaps *this* is it. When all
she's thought of is what you have done and what you are
and how you shall be. Your glory has been all I've lived for.
Say what I ask for is not proper and then turn me back;
then, then you can call yourself honest. Look at him, he
can't even look at me, he turns away . . . The name of
Coriolanus means more to him than ours; so this is the end.
We will get back to Rome, and I with the rest of them. This
boy doesn't know what he's asking for but you'd refuse him
everything. Come, Virgilia. This man's mother must have
been a Volscian, his wife is in Corioli and his child no more
than a stand-up chance. Tell us to go. I shall say nothing
until our city's under fire. Then—then, I'll have things to
say!

(CORIOLANUS *holds his mother by the hand, silent.*)

CORIOLANUS: Oh, Mother, Mother! What have you done? Look, everyone watches this scene and laughs at every single element in it. Oh Mother, Mother! Oh! You've won a skilful victory for Rome, but, for your son, believe it, oh, believe it!—you don't know what you've done to *him*. But perhaps you do, and you were right to have done it. So be it . . . (*to* AUFIDIUS) Aufidius, though I can't make war too well, I can patch up the peace. Tell me, Aufidius, in my place, would you have done less? Or granted less? Aufidius?

AUFIDIUS: I'm most touched.

(*He sounds cold.*)

CORIOLANUS: I dare say. It was no small thing to win me over but you will advise me. I know—I won't go to Rome. I'll stay here with you. We can stick together. Oh, Mother! Virgilia! Soon we will all have a drink together and we'll think about *other* things. We shall not after all be gone forever, in spite of what's happened. Come and have something to eat and drink with us, both of you. You deserve a shrine built to you; all the fire power in Italy and the entire world could not have made this peace . . .

(*They go out.*)

SCENE NINE

Rome. Conference room. MENENIUS *and* SICINIUS. *Enter high-ranking* POLICE OFFICER.

POLICE OFFICER: Sir, I would advise you both to return home while you can. Sicinius, madam, the Plebians have got your fellow tribune and hung him upside down. If Marcius's ladies don't come back with something, things are going to be very bad indeed. He's dying by inches at this moment.

(*Enter another* POLICE OFFICER.)

SICINIUS: Well?

2ND POLICE OFFICER: The news looks good after all. The ladies seem to have had their way. The Volscians are moving out

now, already. There's no Marcius! Rome's even starting to
look a bit like its old self!

SICINIUS: Is this true? Are you certain?

2ND POLICE OFFICER: As certain as one can be, madam. Listen!
(*Sounds of celebration outside.*)

MENENIUS: I'll go and meet Volumnia and the wife. They are
worth all of this, this city, full of politicians like myself, yes,
and tribunes. They must have a real welcome.
(*They go. Noise of celebration grows.*)

SCENE TEN

Corioli. AUFIDIUS's *headquarters.* AUFIDIUS *with* LIEUTENANTS.

AUFIDIUS: Get the others in here. It's him I accuse. Now! Move.
(*Exit* LIEUTENANT, *to be followed by several more entering.*)
Come in.

1ST LIEUTENANT: And how's our general?

AUFIDIUS: Feeling like any man betrayed feels.

2ND LIEUTENANT: The people must know where they are, where
they stand, where *you* stand.

AUFIDIUS: I know. I gambled and I gambled and I gambled!
I seem to be his follower to every one, not partner. It was
as if I'd been a mercenary to a mercenary.

1ST LIEUTENANT: It had to be admitted some time. We all marvelled
at it. And at the very end when we had got Rome itself and
everything was open to us——

AUFIDIUS: That was it. How could I be so weak! Just for a few
tears. I've seen enough. They can be as cheap as lies. He
sold out without an hour's labour. Well, he shall get the
reward. Listen!
(*Outside drums, trumpets and shouts.*)

1ST LIEUTENANT: You slunk into your own time like a nobody and
he comes home the conquering hero.

2ND LIEUTENANT: Do what you feel. We all feel it.

AUFIDIUS: Say no more. Here are the others.

(*Enter various other* OFFICIALS *of the Volscian Army*.)

OFFICIALS: Welcome back.

AUFIDIUS: I don't deserve welcome. Do you know what's happened?

OFFICIALS: We do.

1ST OFFICIAL: There has been a terrible yielding here—and there's no excuse for it.

AUFIDIUS: Here he comes. Hear him for yourself.

(*Enter* CORIOLANUS, *accompanied by drum and colours*.)

CORIOLANUS: My friends! I've come back *and* I'm still one of you. Still unseduced, unseduced by my past loves as when I left you still under your command. . . . As you know, I got us to the gates of Rome itself. We have brought back all kinds of concessions, more than I could ever have hoped for and we've made peace; peace with honour to *us* and what is nothing more than shame to the Romans! See what I've brought back! (*He makes to hand to them a document*.)

AUFIDIUS: Don't read it, my friends. Don't bother to read it. Just tell the traitor how he's abused you all.

CORIOLANUS: Traitor! What's this!

AUFIDIUS: Yes, traitor, Marcius!

CORIOLANUS: Marcius!

AUFIDIUS: Yes, Marcius, Caius Marcius. Do you think I'll let you get away with that name you pilfered, Coriolanus, in Corioli?

CORIOLANUS: You're a true patriot, Aufidius, for a true patriot is a good hater. You come from a good-natured people and you have many virtues but they are of the heart, a cold one too, not of the head. In your passions and affections you are sincere but in understanding; you are all hypocrites, every one. When you begin to calculate the consequences, self-interest prevails over everything. You have wit, genius, eloquence, imagination, affection: but you have no under-standing and consequently no standard of thought or action. Your strength of mind cannot keep up with the pace of your so-called warmth of feeling or your apparent quickness. Your animal spirits run away with you. Oh yes, there is something crude and undigested and discordant in almost everything you do *or* say. You have no system, no abstract ideas. You are everything by starts, and nothing long. You are a wild lot. You hate any law that imposes on your understanding or any kind of restraint at all. You are all fierceness and levity. If you have any feelings, when they aren't excited by novelty or opposition, they grow cold and stagnant. If your blood's not heated by passion, then it turns to poison.

AUFIDIUS: I saw him, I watched him like a twist of rotten silk. He whined and roared away your victory! We all blush to look at him.

CORIOLANUS: Dear God, do you hear this!

AUFIDIUS: Don't bring in God, you boy of tears.

CORIOLANUS: Ha!

AUFIDIUS: No more.

CORIOLANUS: You penurious liar . . . You've made my heart too big! 'Boy!' Oh, you *servant*. Forgive me—this is the first time ever—what you see now *must* give this churlish bitch the lie.

ALL: Cool down, both of you. Let's talk. (*etc.*)

CORIOLANUS: Cut me to pieces, Volscians. Men, and men like children. 'Boy'! You filth in my own place. Yes, me. I was like an eagle in your dovecote. I fluttered your precious Volscians in Corioli! Alone . . . I did it. 'Boy'?

AUFIDIUS: You see!

ALL: Kill him! Put it in! Get on with it! (*etc.*)

(*They all close in on him.*)

CORIOLANUS: Oh, that I had him. With six Aufidiuses and more— his whole tribe. I'd have them ALL!

(AUFIDIUS *howls like a dog and everyone advances on* CORIOLANUS *who is quickly overwhelmed and disappears under the weight of his colours. Presently they all stand back and look upon the body.*)

AUFIDIUS: My friends, you cannot know even in this rage what he did to me, let alone to you. You should be glad he's gone. Even so, he was like some of us, unable to forgive wrongs when they seemed to darken death or night, to defy power, which seems omnipotent . . . neither to change, nor falter, nor repent even this . . . this to him was to be good, great and joyous, beautiful and from this alone, yes, life, joy, empire and victory.

LIEUTENANT: Well, let's make the best of it.

AUFIDIUS (*looking up*): Take him up. Help me, three of you; I'll be one.

(*Sound of a helicopter. Four ropes attached to a stretcher descend from above the proscenium arch.*)

AUFIDIUS: He widowed and unchilded many a one in this city and we're the poorer for it. Still someone may remember. Help me.

(AUFIDIUS *and* THREE LIEUTENANTS *lay the body of* CORIOLANUS *onto the stretcher and cover it with a blanket. It ascends slowly and they watch it and then go out. All that remains on the stage is the lone figure of a piper playing a lament.*)

CURTAIN

THE END